SpringerBriefs in Economics

C000178364

For further volumes:
http://www.springer.com/series/8876

Kjell Hausken • Mthuli Ncube

Quantitative Easing and Its Impact in the US, Japan, the UK and Europe

 Springer

Kjell Hausken
Faculty of Science
University of Stavanger
Stavanger, Norway

Mthuli Ncube
Office of the Chief Economist
African Development Bank Group
Tunis Belvedere, Tunisia

Graduate School of Business
Administration, University of the
Witwatersrand, South Africa

ISSN 2191-5504   ISSN 2191-5512 (electronic)
ISBN 978-1-4614-9645-8   ISBN 978-1-4614-9646-5 (eBook)
DOI 10.1007/978-1-4614-9646-5
Springer New York Heidelberg Dordrecht London

Library of Congress Control Number: 2013955228

Acknowledgment

We thank Qingwei Meng for excellent research assistance.

Acronyms

APP	Asset purchase program
AR	Autoregression
BOE	Bank of England
BOJ	Bank of Japan
BVAR	Bayesian vector autoregression
CBPP	Covered bonds purchase programs
CME	Comprehensive monetary easing
CPI	Consumer price index
EAGB	Euro area government bond
ECB	European Central Bank
ETF	Exchange-traded fund
EUR	Euro
Fed	Federal Reserve System
FOMC	Federal Open Market Committee
FRO	Fixed-rate operation
GBP	British Pound Sterling
GSFF	Growth-supporting funding facility
JGB	Japanese government bond
JPY	Japanese yen
J-REIT	Japan real estate investment trust
LTRO	Longer-term refinancing operation
MBS	Mortgage-backed security
MPC	Monetary Policy Committee
MPM	Monetary Policy Meeting
OAP	Outright asset purchase
OIS	Overnight indexed swap
OMT	Outright monetary transaction
OT	Operation twist
QE	Quantitative easing

QQME   Quantitative and qualitative monetary easing
SFSO   Special fund-supplying operation
SMP   Securities market program
USD   United States dollar
VAR   Vector autoregression
ZIRP   Zero interest rate policy

Contents

Chapter 1
Introduction

Since the advent of the financial crisis in 2008, some of the world's largest central banks, namely the US Federal Reserve (Fed), the Bank of England (BOE), the Bank of Japan (BOJ), and the European Central Bank (ECB), among others, have embarked on monetary easing or quantitative easing. This is an unorthodox way of pumping money into the economy and aiming to lower the long-term interest rates in order to combat a recession. Since interest rates in industrial countries had declined to near zero in the aftermath of the global crisis, the scope for further monetary easing through lower policy rates became very limited. Quantitative easing (QE) and other asset purchase programs have therefore been adopted under exceptional circumstances. Japan is credited as the first country that started implementing QE in 2001. But it was not until the 2008 financial crisis that central banks of developed countries started using QE regularly to stimulate their economies, increase bank lending, and encourage spending. Refer to Tables 4.1, 4.2, 4.3, and 4.4 for a history of QE for the USA, the UK, Japan, and Europe, respectively.

The real estate bubble which burst in 2007 in the USA caused the 2008 financial crisis, and the more recent Eurozone sovereign debt crisis have obliged leading central banks for aggressive monetary actions such as QE in order to prevent financial instability. The USA introduced QE1 in 2008, QE2 in 2010, and "Operation Twist" (OT) in 2011, and more recently the third round of QE (QE3) in 2012, which consisted of a monthly $85 billion injection through the purchase of mortgage-backed securities and longer-term Treasury securities. The Fed buys government or other bonds and then makes this money available for banks to borrow, thereby expanding the amount of money circulating in the economy, which in turn reduces long-term interest rates. In the UK, the BOE incrementally raises the ceiling of its QE asset purchase program to £375 billion, most of which is used to purchase UK government securities. In the euro area, the ECB undertakes a series of longer-term refinancing operations since 2008; two rounds of covered bond purchase programs in 2009 and 2011; an unlimited securities market program in 2010; and open-ended outright monetary transactions in 2012. In Japan, the central bank cumulatively increases the size of its comprehensive monetary easing to as much

K. Hausken and M. Ncube, *Quantitative Easing and Its Impact in the US,*
Japan, the UK and Europe, SpringerBriefs in Economics,
DOI 10.1007/978-1-4614-9646-5_1, © The Author(s) 2013

as ¥101 trillion by the end of 2012. More recently, the BOJ launches perhaps the boldest monetary easing in the modern history with the intention to double the monetary base in 2 years through aggressively purchasing government bonds, exchange-traded funds as well as real estate investment trusts.

Thus, increasing the size of their balance sheets has become the primary means by which central banks in these economies have intervened to bring relief to the ongoing economic downturn. By adopting unconventional measures of monetary easing, central banks seek mainly to stimulate growth, bring down joblessness to reasonable levels and support their banking systems by pumping more money into the economy to boost spending. However, some critics worry that these measures would fuel inflation and encourage unbridled government spending.

The Fed's QE3 is expected to widely affect global economies and this announcement caused euphoria in the financial markets, with stock prices reaching postrecession highs in the USA. In turn, emerging markets received these extraordinary monetary policy responses with skepticism. While central banks in developed economies have deployed monetary easing to ameliorate the impact of the recession, the collective magnitude of monetary easing may have unintended consequences in other countries, especially in emerging countries. As economies are more integrated, the implementation of QE in developed countries can cause excess flow of liquidity in emerging countries and inadvertently disrupt their currencies, exports, and inflation levels.

Looking at the literature, Ugai (2006) presents a survey on the effects of QE policy undertaken by the BOJ from March 2001 through March 2006. The survey shows a clear effect of QE policy in lowering the yield curve centering on the short-to medium-term range through fostering private sector's expectations for the future path of short-term interest rates. During certain phases, the expectations that the zero interest rate would continue into the future was bolstered by increases in the current account balances held by financial institutions at the BOJ. With respect to whether expansion of the monetary base and altering the composition of the BOJ's balance sheet led to portfolio rebalance, the empirical analyses show mixed results. It is believed that the portfolio rebalance effect, if any, was smaller than that stemming from the commitment. As to the impact of QE on Japan's economy through various transmission channels, many of the analyses indicate that the QE created an accommodative environment in terms of corporate financing by containing financial institutions' funding costs from the market and staving off financial institutions' funding uncertainties. The effect of QE on raising aggregate demand and prices, however, was often limited, which was due largely to the structural adjustment in corporate sector, as well as the zero-bound constraint on interest rates. Kurihara (2006a) analyzes Japan's quantitative easing program and its influence on stock prices for economic recovery. There is much dispute over whether quantitative easing has been effective. Kurihara (2006b) investigates the relationship between Japanese stock prices and macroeconomic factors during the BOJ's QE policy. Empirical analysis shows that interest rates have not impacted Japanese stock prices, but exchange rates and the US stock prices have. Furthermore, the BOJ's policy for overcoming recession and deflation is found to be effective.

In their study, Joyce et al. (2011a, b) examine the effects of the quantitative easing program undertaken by the BOE post 2008. As part of its response to the global banking crisis and a sharp downturn in domestic economy, the BOE instituted a program of large-scale asset purchases in March 2009. The purpose was to inject additional money into the economy and increasing nominal spending growth to a level consistent with meeting the consumer price index (CPI) inflation target in the medium term. Most of the BOE's purchases had been of UK government securities (gilts). The finding by Joyce et al. (2011a, b) suggests that QE may have depressed gilt yields by about 100 basis points. On balance, their evidence seems to suggest that the largest part of the impact of QE came through a portfolio rebalance channel. The wider impact on other asset prices is more difficult to disentangle from other influences, and the initial impact was muted but the overall effects were potentially much larger, though subject to considerable uncertainty.

Krishnamurthy and Vissing-Jorgensen (2011) analyze the effect of the US Federal Reserve's QE program, in the form purchases of long-term Treasuries and other long-term bonds (QE1 in 2008–2009 and QE2 in 2010–2011), on interest rates. Using an event-study methodology, they reach two main findings. First, they find that QE works through several channels that impact particular assets differently. They find stronger evidence for a signaling channel, a unique demand for long-term safe assets, an inflation channel for both QE1 and QE2, a mortgage-backed securities prepayment channel, and a corporate bond default risk channel for QE1. Second, effects on particular assets depend critically on which assets are purchased. Their event-study also suggests that mortgage-backed securities purchases in QE1 were crucial for the lowering of yields on mortgage-backed securities, as well as corporate credit risk and thus corporate yields for QE1, while Treasuries-only purchases in QE2 had a disproportionate effect on Treasuries and agency bonds relative to mortgage-backed securities and corporates. The yields on the latter fell primarily through the market's anticipation of lower future federal funds rates.

The aim of this brief is to analyze, empirically, the effects of QE on interest rates and the economy in the USA, Japan, the UK, and Europe. *First*, we analyze the impact of QE on interest rates by using an event-study methodology focusing on the immediate changes in government bond yields over a fairly narrow interval around the QE-related announcements in order to capture the market's direct reaction to the news released. We then take the cumulative change over all the relevant events as a measure of the overall effects of QE-related announcements on interest rates. The measures undertaken by the Federal Reserve and BOE, which focus primarily on bond purchases, are much more effective in lowering interest rates than those undertaken by the BOJ and ECB, which have relied more heavily on lending to private financial institutions. Although the unconventional monetary policies adopted by the Federal Reserve and BOE are similarly designed and both are proven to be effective, our empirical results show that they affect interest rates through distinct transmission mechanisms. The signaling channel seems more dominant in the QE program conducted by the US Federal Reserve, while the portfolio rebalance channel plays a more important role in the QE program of the BOE. The results also show that, in the UK and the USA, over 80 % of the cumulative changes in government bond yields are attributable to the first around of their QE. The market responses to the subsequent rounds of QE are much less significant. *Second*, we use large Bayesian vector autoregression (BVAR) models to estimate the impact of QE on the wider economy by assuming that the macroeconomic effects of QE work entirely through its impact on government bond yield spreads. More specifically, we produce no-QE counterfactual forecasts using large BVAR models by adjusting the spreads between government bond yields and the 3-month Treasury bill rate based on our empirical findings. The no-QE counterfactuals are then compared with their corresponding baseline forecasts which incorporate the effects of QE on government bond spreads. The difference between the two scenarios is considered as the broader economic impact of the unconventional monetary policies. Our results clearly show that the unconventional monetary measures are effective policy options in supporting price stability. Inflation in the major economies would have been lower or more negative if the unconventional monetary policies had not been undertaken by their central banks. The results also suggest that the effect of QE on economic growth is rather limited. No significant effect of QE on GDP growth is found for the major economies, except for the UK where GDP growth would have been as much as 0.7 % point lower if the BOE had not implemented its unconventional monetary policies. Despite the failure of stimulating economic activities as a whole, our simulation results suggest that the unconventional monetary policies to some extent encourage industrial production in the USA, the UK, and Japan. In addition, our analysis found that QE contributes to the reduction in unemployment in the USA and Japan, and a rise in inflation expectations in the USA, the UK, and Euro area. However, evidence on the QE's effect on house prices, stock prices, consumer confidence, and exchange rate is mixed and thus inconclusive. It does seem monetary policy alone is not enough, without some structural reforms and other policy measures.

For related literature, see Barro and Gordon (1983a), Baumeister and Benati (2010), Beetsma and Jensen (1999), Berkmen (2012), Christensen and Rudebusch (2012), Chung et al. (2012), Clarida et al. (1999), Estrella (2005), Fawley and Neely (2013), Gagnon et al. (2011), Lam (2011), Rogoff (1985), Shirai (2013), Svensson (1997), Ueda (2012), Woodford (1999a), etc.

Chapter 2 shows the channels through which QE impacts the markets and economy. Chapter 3 develops the central bank loss function and quantitative easing as a Stackelberg game. Chapter 4 presents an event study on the impact of QE on interest rates. Chapter 5 presents the impact of QE on the economy and various macroeconomic indicators. Chapter 6 concludes.

Chapter 2
Transmission Channels for QE and Effects on Interest Rates

Recent literature on unconventional monetary policy has identified a number of potential channels through which QE can potentially have an impact on interest rates, which in turn may change the willingness of companies to invest and employ, individuals to spend, and banks to lend (see, for example, Joyce et al. 2011a, b; Krishnamurthy and Vissing-Jorgensen 2011). These changes are then expected to influence the level of inflation and economic growth.

Basically, the purpose of undertaking QE is the same as cutting policy rate. It affects interest rates through various transmission channels. First, by announcing large-scale asset purchases, central banks provide information about the likely path of future monetary policies to market participants through a *signaling channel*. Purchasing a large quantity of long-term assets under QE serves as a credible commitment by central banks to keep interest low in the future. This is because, if the central banks raise interest rate later, they will see huge losses on the assets they purchased under QE. The signaling channel is expected to affect interest rates across the yield curve with effects depending on bond maturities (Krishnamurthy and Vissing-Jorgensen 2011).

Second, by purchasing a large quantity of assets held by the private sector through QE, central banks change the relative supply of the assets being purchased, and thus induce equilibrating changes in their relative yields. Since the base money issued and the financial assets purchased under QE are not perfect substitutes, the sellers of financial assets may attempt to rebalance their portfolios by buying other assets which have similar characteristics to the assets sold. This process, therefore, further pushes up the prices of the assets purchased under QE as well as the prices of their close substitutes, and brings down the associated term premiums and yields. The impact of QE through this *portfolio rebalance channel*, therefore, should be more significant on the prices of assets with characteristics similar to those that the central bank purchases.

Finally, central banks increase the liquidity in the hands of investors by purchasing long-term securities and issuing bank reserves under QE. Joyce et al. (2011a, b) assert that increased liquidity and improved market functioning, as the results of central banks' asset purchases, will lower premium for illiquidity, and thus increase asset prices. On the contrary, Krishnamurthy and Vissing-Jorgensen (2011) argue

K. Hausken and M. Ncube, *Quantitative Easing and Its Impact in the US, Japan, the UK and Europe*, SpringerBriefs in Economics, DOI 10.1007/978-1-4614-9646-5_2, © The Author(s) 2013

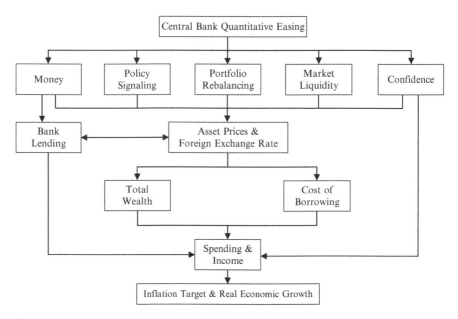

Fig. 2.1 Transmission channels of quantitative easing. *Note*: Adopted from Joyce et al. (2011a, b)

that an expansion in liquidity reduces the liquidity price premium carried by government bonds relative to other less liquid assets and therefore increase government bond yields. However, the effect of QE through the liquidity premia channel may only persist while the central banks are conducting asset purchases.

Large-scale asset purchases financed by central banks under QE, therefore, push up asset prices by lowering expectations about the path of future short rate and reducing term premium. Higher asset prices, on the one hand, increase the net wealth of asset holders, on the other hand, reduce the cost of borrowing. Both the wealth and borrowing cost effects created by QE are expected to boost nominal spending of companies and individuals, so as to achieve inflation target, stimulate real economic growth, and reduce unemployment rate.

Apart from QE working through the asset prices channel, it may also have an impact on inflation and economic growth through bank lending and confidence channels. Since QE improves the liquidity of the banking sector, it encourages banks to finance more new loans than they would have done. But the bank lending channel is expected to have very limited effect given the strains in the financial system in the wake of the crisis. Under such circumstances, banks are more likely to choose to hold central bank injections of money as a cushion rather than pass liquidity onto the real economy through lending. QE is also expected to improve economic outlook and thus have a broader confidence effects. The boosted confidence, on the one hand, may encourage investment and spending directly; on the other hand, it may further increase asset prices by reducing risk premium.

Various channels through which QE may support investment and spending are summarized in Fig. 2.1. In this brief, we highlight the importance of signaling of portfolio rebalancing effects of QE on interest rates with different maturities, which in turn may impact the broader economy.

Chapter 3
The Central Bank Loss Function and Quantitative Easing as a Stackelberg Game

The central bank loss function implies that the central bank's benefit of QE is that of reputation enhancement of controlled inflation and strong economic growth. The loss function equals the sum of the quadratic deviations of the actual inflation and actual GDP from their socially desirable targets, divided by 2. The loss function at any time t is given by

$$L_t = \frac{1}{2}\left[\left(\pi_t - \pi^*\right)^2 + \theta\left(y_t - y^*\right)^2\right],\tag{3.1}$$

where π_t is the actual inflation rate at time t, π^* is the socially desirable and targeted inflation rate, y_t is the actual GDP at time t, and y^* is the social desirable or targeted GDP, and $\theta \geq 0$ is the relative weight placed on output stabilization against inflation stabilization.

Svensson (1997) posits that society minimizes the expected value of some discounted intertemporal loss function into the future, i.e.,

$$E\left(\sum_{t=1}^{\infty}\beta^{t-1}L_t\right),\tag{3.2}$$

where $0 < \beta < 1$ is the discount factor and E is the expectation operator, and L_t is the loss function. When the central bank eases quantitatively, it believes that actual realized inflation in the future will not deviate too much from the target, but output will increase significantly to approach its target. QE is thus stimulatory to the economy.

Consider a Stackelberg game over two time periods with two players which are the central bank and the market. In period 1 the central bank as the leader chooses either quantitative easing (Q) or no quantitative easing (N, i.e., counterfactual). In period 2 the market as the follower chooses either to lower interest rates (L), keep interest rates unchanged (U), or raise interest rates (R). We consider the market as a follower since it consists of a large number of individual economic agents which cannot collectively act strategically through coordination. Instead, each individual

K. Hausken and M. Ncube, *Quantitative Easing and Its Impact in the US, Japan, the UK and Europe*, SpringerBriefs in Economics, DOI 10.1007/978-1-4614-9646-5_3, © The Author(s) 2013

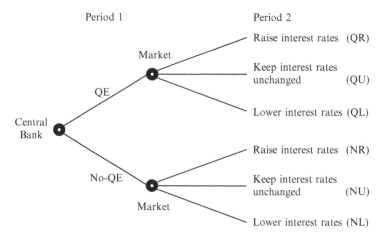

Fig. 3.1 Quantitative easing and interest rate changes as a tree structure for the strategic form two-period game. *Note*: The six outcomes at the right, each expressed with two letters, follow from combining the players' strategies

market participant acts strategically as a follower which jointly causes a collective strategy for the market. The tree structure for the strategic form two-period game is shown in Fig. 3.1. The six outcomes at the right, each expressed with two letters, follow from combining the players' strategies. In this chapter, we illustrate conditions that drive these six outcomes.

To provide intuition for (3.1), assume a typical initial condition of no-QE, desirable inflation ($\pi_t = \pi^*$) and low GDP ($y_t < y^*$). QE beneficially increases y_t towards y^*, thus beneficially lowering L_t. However, QE can cause increased inflation directly and can cause increased interest rates which can also cause increased inflation π_t, thus increasing L_t. Consequently, QE causes decreased loss L_t in (3.1) only when y_t increases so that $(y_t - y^*)^2$ decreases more than $(\pi_t - \pi^*)^2$ increases. Thus QE is a double edged sword. It can beneficially increase GDP, but detrimentally increase inflation.

To link this reasoning to Fig. 2.1, assume that the six outcomes cause six different inflation levels $\pi_{t6} \geq \pi_{t5} \geq \pi_{t4} \geq \pi_{t3} \geq \pi_{t2} \geq \pi_{t1}$ and GDP levels y_t so that the central bank's losses ordinally ranked from 1 to 6 are

$$
\begin{aligned}
E\left(QR : y_t = y^*, \pi_{t6} > \pi^*\right) &\sim 6, \quad M(QR) \sim 6 \\
E\left(QU : y_t = y^*, \pi_{t4} > \pi^*\right) &\sim 4, \quad M(QU) \sim 5 \\
E\left(QL : y_t = y^*, \pi_{t2} > \pi^*\right) &\sim 2, \quad M(QL) \sim 4 \\
E\left(NR : y_t < y^*, \pi_{t5} > \pi^*\right) &\sim 5, \quad M(NR) \sim 3 \\
E\left(NU : y_t < y^*, \pi_{t3} > \pi^*\right) &\sim 3, \quad M(NU) \sim 2 \\
E\left(NL : y_t < y^*, \pi_{t1} > \pi^*\right) &\sim 1, \quad M(NL) \sim 1
\end{aligned}
\tag{3.3}
$$

Table 3.1 Players' common ordinal profits

		Market		
		Lower interest rates	Keep interest rates unchanged	Raise interest rates
Central bank	Quantitative easing	5, 4	3, 5	1, **6**
	No quantitative easing	**6**, 3	**4**, 2	**2**, 1

where M is the market's ordinally ranked profits. Converting losses to profits by reversing the central bank ranking, (3.3) is expressed as Table 3.1, where 6 means most preferred and 1 means least preferred, for the central bank and the market. Bold numbers express preferred profits for each player.

That is, the central bank prefers no-QE over QE, and prefers low interest rates. In contrast, with QE, the market prefers high interest rates expressed with 6, to benefit from the high liquidity, and with no-QE, the market prefers low interest rates expressed with 3, since liquidity is low. The Nash equilibrium in Table 3.1 is (No-QE, Lower interest rates) with payoffs (6, 3). This means that no-QE occurs in equilibrium.

Let us compare Table 3.1 with the data in Table 3.2 below which classifies 69 QE events and 69 no-QE counterfactuals for four central banks, i.e., 17 events for the Federal Reserve, 9 events for Bank of England, 32 events for Bank of Japan, and 11 events for the European Central Bank.

The no-QE counterfactuals in Table 3.2 almost exclusively cause unchanged interest rates. Hence we interchange the profits 2 and 3 for the market as in Table 3.3 causing one Nash equilibrium with payoffs (4, 3) and no-QE.

Since QE indeed occurs in practice, assume that the central bank prefers QE if the market responds by lowering interest rates or keeping interest rates unchanged, but not if the market raises interest rates. This means interchanging 6 and 5 and interchanging 4 and 3 for the central bank causing Table 3.4 which has no Nash equilibrium (no cell has two bold numbers), illustrating the tension between the two players. We get a perpetual dance around the matrix. The central bank chooses QE and we get the upper left cell. Then the market responds by raising interest rates and we get the upper right cell. The central bank then prefers no-QE to earn 2 rather than 1, which gives the lower right cell. The market responds causing $(3, 3) \rightarrow (4, 5) \rightarrow (1, 6) \rightarrow (2, 1) \rightarrow (3, 3) \rightarrow$ etc.

To explain the eight QE events in Table 3.2 where the market responds to QE by raising interest rates, we interchange 2 and 1 for the central bank in Table 3.4 causing Table 3.5 which indeed has a Nash equilibrium in the upper right cell. This outcome occurred only 1 out of 16 times for the Federal Reserve, 3 out of 9 times for BOE, never for BOJ, and 4 out of 11 times for the ECB.

To explain the most common 49 QE events in Table 3.2 where the market responds to QE by keeping interest rates unchanged, we interchange 6 and 5 in Table 3.5 for the market causing Table 3.6 which has a Nash equilibrium in the

Table 3.2 Classification of outcome (frequency and average change in the benchmark 10-year government bond yields)

Central bank	Policy choice	Forecast method	Market		
			Lower interest rates	Keep interest rates unchanged	Raise interest rates
Federal Reserve	QE	–	7 (–27 bps)	9 (–1 bp)	1 (28 bps)
	No-QE	Naïve	0 (N.A.)	17 (0 bp)	0 (N.A.)
		AR(1)	1 (–13 bps)	16 (–1 bp)	0 (N.A.)
		AR(2)	1 (–13 bps)	15 (1 bp)	1 (29 bps)
Bank of	QE	–	3 (–38 bps)	3 (–3 bps)	3 (11 bps)
England	No-QE	Naïve	0 (N.A.)	9 (0 bp)	0 (N.A.)
		AR(1)	0 (N.A.)	9 (0 bp)	0 (N.A.)
		AR(2)	0 (N.A.)	9 (0 bp)	0 (N.A.)
Bank of Japan	QE	–	1 (–10 bps)	31 (–1 bp)	0 (N.A.)
	No-QE	Naïve	0 (N.A.)	32 (0 bp)	0 (N.A.)
		AR(1)	1 (–14 bps)	31 (0 bp)	0 (N.A.)
		AR(2)	0 (N.A.)	32 (–1 bp)	0 (N.A.)
European	QE	–	1 (–16 bps)	6 (0 bp)	4 (10 bps)
Central Bank	No-QE	Naïve	0 (N.A.)	11 (0 bp)	0 (N.A.)
		AR(1)	0 (N.A.)	11 (0 bp)	0 (N.A.)
		AR(2)	0 (N.A.)	11 (0 bp)	0 (N.A.)
Summary of	QE	–	12 (–27 bps)	49 (–1 bp)	8 (13 bps)
outcomes	No-QE	Naïve	0 (N.A.)	69 (0 bp)	0 (N.A.)
		AR(1)	2 (–14 bps)	67 (0 bp)	0 (N.A.)
		AR(2)	1 (–13 bps)	67 (0 bp)	1 (29 bps)

Notes: The classification of QE outcomes and no-QE counterfactuals is based on observed and simulated changes in yield of benchmark 10-year government bond over a 2-day event window, respectively. The frequency of each possible outcome is reported in the corresponding cell alongside the average change in 10-year government bond yield of the events fall into the category. Three forecast methods are used to produce the no-QE counterfactuals for the changes in 10-year government bond yield, namely naïve, AR(1) and AR(2). The methodologies are described in detail in this section. The 5th and 95th percentiles of the distribution of 2-day changes in 10-year government bond yield in normal time (2003–2007) are used as the critical values to classify the QE outcomes and their no-QE counterfactuals

Table 3.3 Players' common ordinal profits

		Market		
		Lower interest rates	Keep interest rates unchanged	Raise interest rates
Central bank	Quantitative easing	5, 4	3, 5	1, **6**
	No quantitative easing	**6**, 2	**4, 3**	**2**, 1

Table 3.4 Players' profits

		Market		
		Lower interest rates	Keep interest rates unchanged	Raise interest rates
Central bank	Quantitative easing	**6**, 4	**4**, 5	1, **6**
	No quantitative easing	5, 2	3, **3**	**2**, 1

Table 3.5 Players' profits

		Market		
		Lower interest rates	Keep interest rates unchanged	Raise interest rates
Central bank	Quantitative easing	**6**, 4	**4**, 5	**2, 6**
	No quantitative easing	5, 2	3, **3**	1, 1

Table 3.6 Players' profits

		Market		
		Lower interest rates	Keep interest rates unchanged	Raise interest rates
Central bank	Quantitative easing	**6**, 4	**4, 6**	**2**, 5
	No quantitative easing	5, 2	3, **3**	1, 1

Table 3.7 Players' profits

		Market		
		Lower interest rates	Keep interest rates unchanged	Raise interest rates
Central bank	Quantitative easing	**6, 6**	**4**, 5	**2**, 4
	No quantitative easing	5, 2	3, **3**	1, 1

upper middle cell. This outcome occurred 9 out of 16 times for the Federal Reserve, 3 out of 9 times for BoE, overwhelmingly 31 out of 32 times for BOJ, and 6 out of 11 times for the ECB.

Finally, to explain the intermediately common 12 QE events in Table 3.2 where the market responds to QE by lowering interest rates, we interchange 6 and 4 in Table 3.5 for the market causing Table 3.7 which has a Nash equilibrium in the upper left cell. This outcome occurred 7 out of 16 times for the Federal Reserve, 3 out of 9 times for BOE, only 1 out of 32 times for BOJ, and only 1 out of 11 times for the ECB.

Chapter 4
The Impact of Quantitative Easing on Interest Rates

In this chapter, we empirically examine the impact of the recent quantitative easing (QE)-related announcements by the Federal Reserve, Bank of England, Bank of Japan, and European Central Bank on their respective government bond yields using an event study methodology. This methodology has been widely used in the recent studies on the similar topics (see, for example, Kapetanios et al. 2012; Christensen and Rudebusch 2012; Joyce et al. 2011a, b; Lam 2011; etc.).[1] Following the literature, our event study focuses on the immediate changes in government bond yields over a fairly narrow interval around the QE-related announcements to capture the market's direct reaction to the news released, and we then take the cumulative change over all the relevant events as a measure of the overall effects of QE-related announcements on interest rates. Given the fundamental differences in both the instruments used and the structures of the economies, interest rates are likely to respond to QE-related announcements in different ways across the economies.

4.1 Event Study Methodology

For the event study, we follow Joyce et al.'s (2011a, b) approach, which has also been adopted by Christensen and Rudebusch (2012) and Kapetanios et al. (2012). The main idea is that QE may affect government bond yields through the signaling channel by influencing the expectations about future short-term interest rates, or through the portfolio rebalance channel by changing the relative supply of particular asset classes. Christensen and Rudebusch (2012) point out that the relative importance of the different channels of QE may depend on market institutional structures and central bank communication policies. To illustrate the research methodology

---

[1] Previous studies, however, reflect only the first waves of the recent QE programs. Little attention has been directed to the comparison of the effectiveness of QE programs over time and across economies.

x

utilized in this chapter, it is useful to briefly recap Joyce et al.'s (2011a, b) approach before we proceed to the empirical analyses.

In an attempt to assess the role of the various channels in affecting interest rates, Joyce et al. (2011a, b) decompose changes in government bond yields around QE-related announcements into two compositions, i.e., changes attributable to lower policy expectation and changes attributable to lower term premiums. Their decomposition relies crucially on interest rates from overnight indexed swap (OIS) contracts.[2] They argue that, because OIS contracts settle on overnight interest rates and only the net difference in interest rates is paid at maturity, OIS rates should therefore incorporate minimal credit risk or counterparty risk. Since the OIS market has developed rapidly and OIS contracts are traded actively in recent years, OIS rates should also have limited liquidity risk. In addition, OIS rates, as a derived contract, are believed to be less sensitive to demand and supply imbalances in the bond market. Thus, it is reasonable to assume that OIS rates provide an accurate proxy for the expected future policy rate which is not subject to default and liquidity risk and less sensitive to supply constraints (Joyce et al. 2011a, b). The movements in OIS rates over the event windows, therefore, reflect changes in risk-adjusted expectation of the average policy rate over the life of the swap contracts attributable to the QE-related announcements, while the movements in the spread between government bond yields and their corresponding OIS rates represent the combined effect of QE through both the portfolio rebalance and liquidity channels.

More precisely, government bond yields can be expressed by the sum of expected future short rates and the term premium as follows:

$$y(GB)_t^n = (1/n)\sum_{i=0}^{n-1} E_t r_{t+i} + TP(GB)_t^n \tag{4.1}$$

where $y(GB)_t^n$ is the yield on government bond with an n-period maturity at time t; $E_t r_{t+i}$ denotes the expected one-period (risk-free) short rate for $t+i$ at time t; and $TP(GB)_t^n$ represents the term premium associated with the n-period government bond at time t. According to Joyce et al. (2011a, b), the term premium on government bond can be further decomposed into two elements, namely, an instrument-specific premium and a future short rates uncertainty premium,

$$TP(GB)_t^n = TP1(GB)_t^n + TP2(GB)_t^n \tag{4.2}$$

where $TP1(GB)_t^n$ represents an instrument-specific effect that captures bond-specific credit and liquidity premium as well as any effects from demand and supply imbalances; and $TP2(GB)_t^n$ denotes a term premium element that reflects uncertainty about future short rates. If the credit premium on government bond can be assumed

---

[2] An OIS contract involves the exchange of a predefined (fixed) OIS rate based on a specific currency with one linked to a compounded (floating) overnight interbank interest rate that prevails over the life of the swap contract. In the absence of arbitrage, OIS rates reflect risk-adjusted expectations of the average policy rate over the horizon corresponding to the maturity of the swap.

to be negligible, the movements in the instrument-specific premium $(TP1(GB)_t^n)$ reflect either changes in liquidity premium or demand and supply effects from QE that come through the portfolio rebalance channel (Joyce et al. 2011a, b).[3]

Similarly, the interest rates from OIS contracts can also be decomposed as follows:

$$y\left(OIS\right)_t^n = \left(1/n\right)\sum_{i=0}^{n-1}E_t r_{t+i} + TP\left(OIS\right)_t^n \qquad (4.3)$$

where $y(OIS)_t^n$ is the interest rate from the n-period maturity OIS contract at time t; $E_t r_{t+i}$ is the one-period short (risk-free) rate; and $TP(OIS)_t^n$ denotes the term premium associated with the n-period OIS rate. In principle, the term premium associated with OIS rates can be broken down into an instrument-specific premium and a conventional term premium,

$$TP\left(OIS\right)_t^n = TP1\left(OIS\right)_t^n + TP2\left(OIS\right)_t^n \qquad (4.4)$$

where $TP1(OIS)_t^n$ represents an instrument-specific premium that captures credit and liquidity premium as well as any effects from demand and supply imbalances; and $TP2(OIS)_t^n$ denotes a conventional term premium that reflects uncertainty about future short rates. As argued by Joyce et al. (2011a, b), the first element of the term premium associated with OIS rates $TP1(OIS)_t^n$ is negligible, and thus the movements in OIS term premium $TP(OIS)_t^n$ reflect perceived uncertainty about the future short rates rather than liquidity or credit premium or effects from demand and supply imbalances. In other words, the term premium associated with an OIS rate is equivalent to the future short rate uncertainty premium in the corresponding maturity-matched government bond yield, and thus

$$TP\left(OIS\right)_t^n = TP2\left(OIS\right)_t^n = TP2\left(GB\right)_t^n \qquad (4.5)$$

Based on this assumption, the movements in the spread between government bond yields and their corresponding maturity-matched OIS rates should be able to capture the changes in the government bond-specific premium and, therefore, the impact of QE on government bond yields through the portfolio rebalance channel. It is worth mentioning that this approach may, to some extent, underestimate the importance of the portfolio rebalance channel if the OIS rates are also driven by the same factors influencing bond-specific premium such as demand and supply imbalances (Joyce et al. 2011a, b). Besides, OIS rates from derived contracts may have their own set of risk premiums and thus are not perfect measures of the expected future short rates (Christensen and Rudebusch 2012).

---

[3] Joyce et al. (2011a, b) examine separate evidence on market functioning (e.g., bid-ask spreads) to identify the role of the liquidity premium channel, but the importance of this channel appears to be small in the context of gilts. Accordingly, they argue that more emphasis can be placed on the relative importance of portfolio rebalance effects in driving bond-specific premium around QE-related announcements.

4.2 QE-Related Events

To carry out the event study, we identify a set of key announcements regarding the unconventional monetary policies for each of the advanced economies under investigation. The event set regarding the US Federal Reserve's unconventional monetary policies includes the large-scale asset purchase programs (APPs), i.e., QE1, QE2, and QE3, as well as the maturity extension program, i.e., operation twist (OT) (see Table 4.1 for the full list of the Federal Reserve's QE-related event dates). The first eight events listed in Table 4.1 are comparable to those identified in Gagnon et al. (2011), which focuses on the effect of the first round of QE by the Federal Reserve from November 2008 to the fall of 2009.[4] In addition, we update Gagnon et al.'s (2011) event set by including the subsequent announcements of QE2 and QE3 as well as the implementation of OT, from August 2010 to the end of 2012. The expanded event set enables us to investigate the overall effects of the unconventional measures having thus far been taken by the Federal Reserve. The total number of events in our event set for the USA, therefore, increases to 17 as listed in Table 4.1.

Table 4.2 lists a set of key announcements regarding the Bank of England's programs of large-scale asset purchases, which are known as QE1, QE2, and QE3. The first six events listed in Table 4.2 are identical with the events examined in Joyce et al. (2011a, b) and Christensen and Rudebusch (2012). Again, we further incorporate the Bank of England's recent announcements regarding the second and third rounds of QE from October 2011 to July 2012. There are nine events associated with the Bank of England's unconventional monetary policies to be investigated in this brief.

The Bank of Japan has a long history of undertaking QE measures since falling into the prolonged mild deflation phase in the early 2000s. It pioneers the unconventional monetary easing framework in March 2001, in an attempt to stem the continuous price decline and to set the basis for economic growth (see Shirai 2013). Under such a framework, the operating target for the outstanding balance of current account held by financial institutions at the Bank of Japan is incrementally raised to around ¥30 trillion to ¥35 trillion. In 2006, the Bank of Japan finally decides to exit its QE framework and reintroduces the standard uncollateralized overnight call rate as an operating target for money market operations. The effectiveness of QE as a policy instrument, however, remains inconclusive (see, for example, Ugai 2006). Although it is not the focus of this brief, a timeline showing the Bank of Japan's QE-related announcements in the first half of the 2000s is offered in Appendix A.

In response to the recent financial crisis and global recession triggered by the bankruptcy of Lehman Brothers, the Bank of Japan starts its second round of monetary easing in the late 2009 and subsequently carries out the special fund-supplying operations (SFSOs), outright asset purchases (OAPs), fixed-rate operations (FROs), fixed-rate funds-supplying operations (FRFSO), growth-supporting funding facility (GSFF), comprehensive monetary easing (CME), and quantitative and qualitative monetary easing (QQME). Table 4.3 summarizes 32 QE-related announcements made by the

---

[4] Krishnamurthy and Vissing-Jorgensen (2011), however, concentrate only on the first five events by arguing that only small yield changes occur on the three later events.

Table 4.1 Federal Reserve's QE-related events

No.	Date	Program	Event	QE-related news	Outcome
1	November 25, 2008	QE1	FOMC statement	Fed intends to purchase up to $500 billion of agency mortgage-backed securities (MBSs) and up to $100 billion of agency debt	QL
2	December 1, 2008	QE1	Bernanke speech	Fed may purchase long-term Treasury or agency securities in substantial quantities	QL
3	December 16, 2008	QE1	FOMC statement	Fed mentions possible purchase of long-term Treasuries	QL
4	January 28, 2009	QE1	FOMC statement	Fed stands ready to expand agency debt and MBS purchases and purchase long-term Treasuries	QR
5	March 18, 2009	QE1	FOMC statement	FOMC decides to increase the maximum purchases of agency MBSs and debt to $1.25 trillion and $200 billion, respectively; and to purchase up to $300 billion of longer-term Treasuries	QL
6	August 12, 2009	QE1	FOMC statement	Fed slows the pace of the LSAP by extending purchasing period	QU
7	September 23, 2009	QE1	FOMC statement	Fed slows the pace of agency debt and MBS purchases	QU
8	November 4, 2009	QE1	FOMC statement	Fed downsizes the amount of agency debt purchase to $175 billion instead of the $200 billion	QU
9	August 10, 2010	QE1	FOMC statement	Fed decides to keep constant its holdings of securities at current level by reinvesting principal payments from agency debt and agency MBSs in longer-term Treasuries	QL
10	August 27, 2010	QE2	Bernanke speech	Bernanke hints at QE2 in his speech at Federal Reserve Bank of Kansas City Symposium	QU
11	September 21, 2010	QE2	FOMC statement	FOMC reiterates its intention to maintain its policy using new language with added emphasis	QL

(continued)

Table 4.1 (continued)

No.	Date	Program	Event	QE-related news	Outcome
12	November 3, 2010	QE2	FOMC statement	Fed intends to further purchase $600 billion in longer-term Treasury securities	QU
13	September 21, 2011	OT	FOMC statement	Fed intends to purchase $400 billion in Treasuries with remaining maturities of 6–30 years and to sell an equal amount of Treasuries with remaining maturities of 3 years or less	QL
14	June 20, 2012	OT	FOMC statement	FOMC expands the operation twist program by adding additionally $267 billion	QU
15	August 22, 2012	QE3	FOMC statement	FOMC members judge that additional monetary accommodation is likely	QU
16	September 13, 2012	QE3	FOMC statement	Fed launches a new $40 billion per month, open-ended, purchasing program of agency MBSs	QU
17	December 12, 2012	QE3	FOMC statement	Fed would purchase longer-term Treasury securities at a pace of $45 billion per month	QU

Source: Authors' summary based on the information provided by the Board of Governors of the Federal Reserve System (http://www.federalreserve.gov/monetarypolicy/fomccalendars.htm)
Notes: QE1, QE2, and QE3 represent the first, second, and third rounds of the Fed's quantitative easing, respectively; and OT represents operation twist. The Fed and FOMC are the Federal Reserve and Federal Open Market Committee, respectively. QL, QU, and QR represent lowered, unchanged, and rising interest rates around QE-related events, respectively

Bank of Japan since 2009 to the present, including the recent dramatic moves in response to Prime Minister Shinzo Abe's call for a target of 2 % of inflation. Our comprehensive event set for Japan covers all important announcements related to the Bank of Japan's QE polices identified in Lam (2011) and Fawley and Neely (2013).

Since the advent of the financial crisis in 2008, the European Central Bank has also implemented a series of unconventional monetary policies in the euro area, including the longer-term refinancing operations (LTROs), covered bonds purchase programs (CBPPs), securities markets program (SMP), and outright monetary trans- actions (OMTs). It is worth noting that assets purchased by the European Central Bank under its SMP and OMTs are sterilized and directed to address the malfunction- ing of securities markets, and thus do not increase the monetary base. Therefore, the unconventional monetary policy measures, such as SMP and OMTs, do not fall under the usual definition of QE. Table 4.4 summarizes the relevant events for the euro area which represent an extension of those identified in Fawley and Neely (2013).

Table 4.2 Bank of England's QE-related events

No.	Date	Program	Event	QE-related news	Outcome
1	February 11, 2009	QE1	Inflation report	The released report and the associated press conference give strong indication that QE is likely	QL
2	March 5, 2009	QE1	MPC statement	BOE would purchase £75 billion of assets funded by central bank reserves. Gilt purchases are likely to be restricted to bonds with a residual maturity of between 5 and 25 years	QL
3	May 7, 2009	QE1	MPC statement	BOE extends the amount of QE asset purchases by a further £50 billion to £125 billion	QR
4	August 6, 2009	QE1	MPC statement	The amount of QE asset purchases is extended by a further £50 billion to £175 billion and the buying range is also extended to gilts with a residual maturity greater than 3 years	QU
5	November 5, 2009	QE1	MPC statement	The amount of QE asset purchases is extended by a further £25 billion to £200 billion	QR
6	February 4, 2010	QE1	MPC statement	The amount of QE asset purchases would be maintained at £200 billion	QU
7	October 6, 2011	QE2	MPC statement	MPC undertakes a further £75 billion of gilt purchases, taking the total to £275 billion	QR
8	February 9, 2012	QE2	MPC statement	MPC increases the size of its asset purchase program (APP) by £50 billion to a total of £325 billion	QU
9	July 5, 2012	QE3	MPC statement	BOE decides to purchase a further £50 billion to bring total asset purchases to £375 billion	QL

Source: Authors' summary based on the information provided by the Bank of England (http://www.bankofengland.co.uk/markets/Pages/sterlingoperations/timeline)

Notes: QE1 and QE2 represent the first and second rounds of the Bank of England's quantitative easing, respectively. BOE and MPC are the Bank of England and its Monetary Policy Committee, respectively. QL, QU, and QR represent lowered, unchanged, and rising interest rates around QE-related events, respectively

Table 4.3 Bank of Japan's QE-related events

No.	Date	Program	Event	QE-related news	Outcome
1	December 2, 2008	SFSO	MPM decisions[a]	BOJ introduces special funds-supplying operations	QU
2	December 19, 2008	OAP	MPM decisions	BOJ decides to increase asset purchases of JGBs from ¥14.4 trillion to ¥16.8 trillion per year	QU
3	January 22, 2009	OAP	MPM decisions	BOJ decides to begin outright purchases of commercial paper and asset-backed commercial paper, and to expand the range of JGBs accepted in outright purchases	QU
4	February 3, 2009	OAP	MPM decisions	BOJ resumes purchases of stocks held by financial institutions	QU
5	February 19, 2009	SFSO/ OAP	MPM decisions	BOJ expands special funds-supplying operations and outright purchases of commercial paper, and begins outright purchases of corporate bonds	QU
6	March 18, 2009	OAP	MPM decisions	BOJ increases its outright purchases of JGBs from ¥16.8 trillion to ¥21.6 trillion per year	QU
7	July 15, 2009	SFSO/ OAP	MPM decisions	BOJ extends the period for outright asset purchases and special funds-supplying operations	QU
8	October 30, 2009	SFSO/ FRO	MPM decisions	BOJ extends its special funds-supplying operations, and intends to provide ample liquidity funds-supplying operation against pooled collateral	QU
9	December 1, 2009	FRO	MPM decisions[a]	BOJ adopts a 3-month funds-supplying operation at the fixed target interest rate of 0.1 % against pooled collateral up to a total amount of ¥10 trillion	QU

(continued)

Table 4.3 (continued)

No.	Date	Program	Event	QE-related news	Outcome
10	December 18, 2009	PST	MPM decisions	The Policy Board clarifies the expression of the "understanding of medium- to long-term price stability" by eliminating the possibility of 0 % price change	QU
11	March 17, 2010	FRO	MPM decisions	The Policy Board increases the amount of the fixed-rate 3-month operation to ¥20 trillion	QU
12	April 30, 2010	GSFF	MPM decisions	The Policy Board indicates further possible ways to provide funds for private financial institutions	QU
13	May 21, 2010	GSFF	MPM decisions	BOJ decides to compile and announce a preliminary framework for fund provisioning	QU
14	June 15, 2010	GSFF	MPM decisions	BOJ introduces the fund-provisioning measure to support strengthening the foundations for economic growth. The maximum amount of funds available under this facility is ¥3 trillion	QU
15	August 30, 2010	FRO	MPM decisions[a]	BOJ introduces a 6-month term in the fixed-rate fund-supplying operation against pooled collateral with a maximum amount of ¥10 trillion	QU
16	October 5, 2010	CME	MPM decisions	BOJ implements a comprehensive monetary easing policy by establishing an APP to purchase financial assets and conduct fixed-rate funds-supplying operations	QL
17	October 28, 2010	CME	MPM decisions	BOJ releases operational details of the APP with a total amount of ¥35 trillion	QU
18	November 5, 2010	CME	MPM decisions	BOJ releases operational details of purchases of exchange-traded funds (ETFs) and Japan real estate investment trusts (J-REITs)	QU

(continued)

Table 4.3 (continued)

No.	Date	Program	Event	QE-related news	Outcome
19	March 14, 2011	CME	MPM decisions	The Policy Board increases the amount of APP by about ¥5 trillion to about ¥40 trillion in total	QU
20	April 28, 2011	DA	MPM decisions	BOJ establishes a funds-supplying operation to support financial institutions in disaster areas with a total amount of loans of ¥1 trillion	QU
21	June 14, 2011	GSFF	MPM decisions	BOJ establishes a new line of credit for equity investment and asset-based lending with a total amount of loans of ¥500 billion	QU
22	August 4, 2011	CME	MPM decisions	The Bank expands the total size of APP by about ¥10 trillion from ¥40 trillion to about ¥50 trillion	QU
23	October 27, 2011	CME	MPM decisions	BOJ further expands the amount of APP by purchasing an additional ¥5 trillion in JGBs	QU
24	February 14, 2012	CME	MPM decisions	BOJ decides to increase the total size of the APP by purchasing an additional ¥10 trillion in JGBs	QU
25	March 13, 2012	GSFF	MPM decisions	The Policy Board increases the growth-supporting funding facility by ¥2 trillion to ¥5.5 trillion	QU
26	April 27, 2012	CME	MPM decisions	The Policy Board increases the total size of APP by about ¥5 trillion, from about ¥65 trillion to about ¥70 trillion	QU
27	July 12, 2012	CME	MPM decisions	BOJ reduces the amount of the fixed-rate funds-supplying operation against pooled collateral by about ¥5 trillion and increases the outright purchases of Treasury discount bills by about ¥5 trillion	QU

(continued)

Table 4.3 (continued)

No.	Date	Program	Event	QE-related news	Outcome
28	September 19, 2012	CME	MPM decisions	The Policy Board decides to increase the size of APP by purchasing about ¥5 trillion in Treasury discount bills and about ¥5 trillion in JGBs	QU
29	October 30, 2012	CME/ SBLF	MPM decisions	The Bank expands the size of APP by about ¥11 trillion, and decides to provide unlimited long-term funds at a low interest rate to financial institutions through a stimulating bank lending facility	QU
30	December 20, 2012	CME/ SBLF	MPM decisions	BOJ increases the size of APP by about ¥10 trillion, from about ¥91 trillion to about ¥101 trillion. The Bank also releases operational details of the unlimited stimulating bank lending facility	QU
31	January 22, 2013	CME	MPM decisions	BOJ raises its price stability target to 2 %, and introduces the open-ended asset purchasing method to its APP	QU
32	April 4, 2013	QQME	MPM decisions	BOJ introduces the quantitative and qualitative monetary easing, under which its main operating target for money market operations is changed to the monetary base. The Bank intends to double the monetary base and the amounts of outstanding JGBs as well as ETFs in 2 years	QU

Source: Authors' summary based on the information provided by the Bank of Japan (http://www.boj.or.jp/en/announcements/index.htm)

Notes: SFSO represents special fund-supplying operation; OAP represents outright asset purchase; FRO represents fixed-rate operation; PST represents price stability target; GSFF represents growth-supporting funding facility; CME represents comprehensive monetary easing; and SBLF represents simulating bank lending facility. BOJ and MPM are the Bank of Japan and its Monetary Policy Meeting; and [a] indicates unscheduled MPM. QL, QU, and QR represent lowered, unchanged, and rising interest rates around QE-related events, respectively

Table 4.4 European Central Bank's QE-related events

No.	Date	Program	Event	QE-related announcement	Outcome
1	March 28, 2008	LTRO	GC Press release	GC decides to conduct supplementary longer-term refinancing operations with a maturity of 6 months	QU
2	October 15, 2008	LTRO	GC Press release	GC decides to conduct all refinancing operations with a fixed-rate tender procedure and full allotment. The list of assets eligible as collectoral is expanded	QU
3	May 7, 2009	LTRO/ CBPP	GC Press release	GC decides to conduct longer-term refinancing operations with a maturity of 12 months, and to purchase euro-denominated covered bonds issued in the euro area	QR
4	June 4, 2009	CBPP	GC Press release	GC releases the technical modalities of the €60 billion covered bonds purchase programs	QR
5	May 10, 2010	SMP	GC Press release	GC decides to conduct interventions in the euro area public and private debt securities markets	QU
6	June 30, 2010	CBPP	GC Press release	The purchases of €60 billion in covered bonds are fully implemented. The Eurosystem central banks intend to keep the purchased covered bonds until maturity	QU
7	October 6, 2011	CBPP	GC Press release	GC decides to launch a new covered bonds purchase programs with an intended amount of €40 billion	QU
8	November 3, 2011	CBPP	GC Press release	GC releases details of the new covered bonds purchase programs. Covered bonds to be purchased under the new program must have a maximum residual of 10.5 years	QR

(continued)

Table 4.4 (continued)

No.	Date	Program	Event	QE-related announcement	Outcome
9	December 8, 2011	LTRO	GC Press release	GC decides to conduct LTROs with a maturity of 36 months, and further expands eligible collectoral	QR
10	August 2, 2012	OMT	ECB Press conference	Draghi indicates the expansion of sovereign debt purchases	QU
11	September 6, 2012	OMT	GC Press release	GC introduces outright monetary transactions with no ex-ante time or size limit	QL

Source: Authors' summary based on the information provided by the European Central Bank (http://www.ecb.europa.eu/press/html/index.en.html)
Notes: LTRO represents longer-term refinancing operation; CBPP represents covered bonds purchase programs; SMP represents securities markets program; and OMT represents outright monetary transaction. ECB and GC are the European Central Bank and its Governing Council, respectively. QL, QU, and QR represent lowered, unchanged, and rising interest rates around QE-related events, respectively

The events listed in Tables 4.1, 4.2, 4.3, and 4.4 cover all the major QE-related announcements made by the central banks. However, it is possible that some other news releases which are omitted here may also be potentially relevant. As indicated in Krishnamurthy and Vissing-Jorgensen (2011), omitting potentially relevant events could lead to an upward or a downward bias, depending on how the events on the omitted days affect the market's expectations of future policies. This methodological limitation, therefore, should be kept in mind when we interpret our empirical results.

4.3 Event Window

To empirically assess the impact of QE on interest rates, we are also confronted with the selecting of window length to be used in our analyses. As argued in Joyce et al. (2011a, b), if the event windows are too short, there is a risk of missing the full market reaction, as it may take time for the market to evaluate the news about the unorthodox monetary policy measures, while, if too long, there is a risk of the estimated reaction being contaminated by other news events as a wide range of other policies released both at home and abroad over the same period may also have significant influences on asset prices. Joyce et al. (2011a, b), therefore, choose a 2-day window for their study on the impact of the Bank of England's QE policy on UK gilts. Meanwhile, they use 1- and 3-day windows to check the robustness of their results. The 2-day event window has also been used by Krishnamurthy and

Vissing-Jorgensen (2011) to evaluate the effect of the Federal Reserve's purchase of long-term Treasuries and other long-term bonds.[5]

Gagnon et al. (2011) and Christensen and Rudebusch (2012) choose to focus on 1-day intervals around the QE-related announcements. However, Christensen and Rudebusch (2012) acknowledge that the 1-day event window, on the one hand, may be too short to capture the full announcement effects; and, on the other hand, may capture an exaggerated initial market response that is unwound over times as market participants adjust. Gagnon et al. (2011) also note that, given the relative novelty of the large-scale asset purchases and the diversity of beliefs about the mechanisms by which they operate, changes may have been absorbed more slowly than for typical monetary policy shocks such as those to the policy rate.

By trading off between allowing sufficient time for revised expectations to become fully incorporated in asset prices and keeping the window narrow enough to make it unlikely to contain the release of other important information, we consider the response of interest rates using a 2-day window around the QE-related announcements, measured from their closing level the day prior to the announcement $(t-1)$ to their closing level the day after the announcement $(t+1)$. In addition, we also use a 1-day event window (between $t-1$ and t) as robustness checks.[6]

4.4   Outcome Classification

To classify the outcomes of the QE-related events according to Fig. 3.1, we focus on the changes in yield of benchmark 10-year government bond over each of the event windows, and compare them with critical values calculated from the distribution of changes in 10-year government bond yield in normal time. More specifically, we consider 2003–2007 to be normal time, and compute the 0.5th, 2.5th, and 5th percentiles at both the top and bottom of the distribution of changes in the 10-year government bond yield over this period of time. For each of the four economies under investigation, we define the changes in 10-year government bond yield which are more negative than the 5th percentile of the distribution in normal time as QL (QE, Lower interest rates, see Fig. 3.1); the changes which are greater than the 95th percentile as QR (QE, Raise interest rates, see Fig. 3.1); and otherwise as QU (QE, Keep interest rates unchanged, see Fig. 3.1). The classification of observed market responses to the QE-related is reported in Tables 4.1, 4.2, 4.3, and 4.4, where the outcome in the rightmost column is one of the six outcomes in Fig. 3.1.

---

[5]Krishnamurthy and Vissing-Jorgensen (2011) find that, for high-liquidity assets such as Treasuries, 2-day changes are almost the same as 1-day changes. For low-liquidity assets, the 2-day changes are almost always larger than the 1-day changes.

[6]By assuming that the entire announcement is a complete surprise, the event study methodology adopted in this brief is likely to underestimate the market response. Christensen and Rudebusch (2012) argue that the later announcements regarding the first round of the Federal Reserve's QE may have been widely anticipated by the market participants.

In addition, we use a number of univariate time series models to produce no-QE counterfactuals for the changes in the 10-year government bond yields over the QE-related windows. The no-QE counterfactuals attempt to show what would have happened to the interest rates had there been no-QE-related announcements. Three forecasting methods are used to produce such no-QE counterfactuals. First, we use a naïve forecast method by assuming that the entire change in the benchmark 10-year government bond yield within an event window is attributable to the QE-related announcement. Under this naïve assumption, there would have been no change if QE had not been announced. Accordingly, the expected value of yield can be expressed as follows:

$$E\left(y\left(GB\right)_t^{10}\right) = y\left(GB\right)_{t-1}^{10} \qquad (4.6)$$

where E represents expected value and $y(GB)_t^{10}$ represents yield of benchmark 10-year government bond at time t. According to (4.6), the expected changes in 10-year government bond yield should always be zero. Such a naïve forecast method is optimal if $y(GB)^{10}$ follows a random walk process.

Second, since government bond yield may exhibit mean reversion, it is plausible to generate no-QE counterfactuals using an autoregressive model. Specifically, we specify an autoregressive model of order 1, i.e., AR(1), for the yield of benchmark 10-year government bond as follows:

$$y\left(GB\right)_t^{10} = \varphi_0 + \varphi_1 y\left(GB\right)_{t-1}^{10} + \varepsilon_t \qquad (4.7)$$

where φ_0 and φ_1 are coefficients, and ε_t is the error term. The autoregressive model is repeatedly estimated using 20 daily observations prior to each of the QE-related events, and then used to forecast the 10-year government bond yield over the event window. We consider the difference between the predicted $y(GB)^{10}$ at the end of the event window and the actual value of $y(GB)^{10}$ observed prior to the event window as the no-QE counterfactual for the event.[7]

Third, instead of modeling the 10-year government bond yield itself, we also estimate an autoregressive model for the series of changes in 10-year government bond yield. Given that 2-day event windows are used in our event study, we forecast changes in 10-year government bond yield by estimating an AR(2) model which is specified as follows:

$$\Delta2\left(y\left(GB\right)^{10}\right)_t = \phi_0 + \phi_1\Delta2\left(y\left(GB\right)^{10}\right)_{t-1} + \phi_2\Delta2\left(y\left(GB\right)^{10}\right)_{t-2} + u_t \qquad (4.8)$$

where $\Delta2$ represents the difference between a value and its two-period lag; ϕ_0, ϕ_1, and ϕ_2 are coefficients; and u_t is the error term. Again, (4.8) is estimated repeatedly

---

[7] In alternative estimates, we specify autoregressive models with higher orders for $y(GB)^{10}$. The higher order autoregressive terms, however, are jointly insignificant in most of the cases, and thus we ignore them in the final estimates.

using 20 daily observations prior to each of the QE-related events. The estimated coefficients are then used to produce an out-of-sample forecast. The predicted changes in 10-year government bond yields over the QE-related event windows are taken as an alternative measure of the no-QE counterfactuals.

The estimated no-QE counterfactuals are also compared with the 5th and 95th percentiles of the distribution of changes in 10-year government bond yield in normal time, and classified as follows. The no-QE counterfactuals which are more negative than the 5th percentile of the distribution are categorized as NL (No-QE, Lower interest rates, see Fig. 3.1); those that exceed the 95th percentile are categorized as NR (No-QE, Raise interest rates, see Fig. 3.1); and otherwise as NU (No-QE, Keep interest rates unchanged, see Fig. 3.1). The no-QE counterfactuals for the changes in 10-year government bond yield over the QE-related event windows are also summarized in Table 3.2.

4.5   Empirical Results

In this section, we report the empirical evidence on the effect of QE-related announcements by central banks on government bond yields in their respective economies. Given the fact that the Federal Reserve and Bank of England's QE programs, which primarily concentrate on bond purchases, are fundamentally different from those of the Bank of Japan and European Central Banks, which rely more heavily on direct lending to the banking sector,[8] interest rate responses to the QE-related announcements are likely to be different across these economies. Moreover, even if the QE programs are similarly designed and operated, the QE-related announcements are likely to affect interest rates through different transmission channels across economies depending on their market institutional structures and central bank communication policies (see Christensen and Rudebusch 2012).

4.5.1   Evidence from the USA

4.5.1.1   The US Treasury Yields (November 1, 2008–December 31, 2012)

Figure 4.1 depicts the movements in the yields of the US government securities (the US Treasuries) at different maturities over the period from November 2008 to December 2012. The vertical lines represent the Federal Reserve's QE-related

---

[8] Fawley and Neely (2013) argue that bond markets play a relatively more important role than banks in the US and UK economies, while banks play a relatively more important role in continental Europe and Japan. Each central bank chooses methods to provide liquidity and support the financial system that reflect the structure of its respective economy.

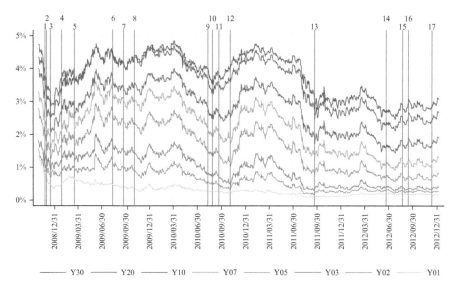

Fig. 4.1 The US Treasury yields at different maturities. *Sources*: Treasury yields are obtained from the FRED. *Note*: *Vertical lines* represent the Fed's QE-related events listed in Table **4.1**

announcements included in our event set for the USA. Comparing their levels at the end of 2012 to those before the start of QE in 2008 suggests that the US Treasury yields reduce significantly at all maturities. The decline in yields is particularly noticeable for those associated with longer-term Treasuries. The overall change in Treasury yields over the entire period, however, is unlikely to provide a good measure of the impact of QE, given the amount of other news which is released over the same period (Joyce et al. 2011a, b). In order to isolate the impact that is directly attributable to the Federal Reserve's unconventional monetary policies, we examine the reaction of the US Treasury yields over a 2-day event window around each QE-related announcement listed in Table 4.1.

4.5.1.2 Fed's QE1-Related Events (Events 1–9)

On November 25, 2008, the Federal Reserve announces that it would purchase up to $100 billion of housing-related government-sponsored enterprises debt (such as direct obligations of Fannie Mae and Freddie Mac) as well as up to $500 billion mortgage-backed securities (MBSs) that these enterprises sponsored. The goal is to lower borrowing costs and to directly ease credit conditions in the housing market, which in turn are expected to support housing market and foster improved conditions in financial markets more generally. Figures reported in Table 4.5 show that the US Treasury yields fall sharply at almost all maturities after this announcement, meanwhile their corresponding US OIS rates fall with similar magnitudes, suggesting that the declines in Treasury yields and OIS rates are driven by a common factor.

Table 4.5 Two-day changes in the US Treasury yields, OIS rates and yield-OIS spreads

Event date	Change	1-year	2-year	3-year	5-year	7-year	10-year	20-year	30-year
1. November 25, 2008 (QE1)	Δ(US Treasury yield)	-2	-22	-15	-23	-28	-36***	-24	-24
	Δ(OIS rate)	-5	-12	-19	-26	-38	-39	-30	-31
	Δ(Yield-OIS spread)	3	-10	4	3	10	3	6	7
2. December 1, 2008 (QE1)	Δ(US Treasury yield)	-13	-10	-15	-28	-27	-25***	-24	-27
	Δ(OIS rate)	-8	-17	-22	-31	-24	-22	-23	-25
	Δ(Yield-OIS spread)	-5	7	7	3	-3	-3	-1	-2
3. December 16, 2008 (QE1)	Δ(US Treasury yield)	-5	-2	-4	-15	-22	-33***	-28	-32
	Δ(OIS rate)	-9	-5	-12	-22	-21	-29	-23	-20
	Δ(Yield-OIS spread)	4	3	8	7	-1	-4	-5	-12
4. January 28, 2009 (QE1)	Δ(US Treasury yield)	4	8	19	28	29	28***	28	31
	Δ(OIS rate)	5	13	21	29	28	37	38	38
	Δ(Yield-OIS spread)	-1	-5	-2	-1	1	-9	-10	-7
5. March 18, 2009 (QE1)	Δ(US Treasury yield)	-9	-18	-24	-36	-47	-41***	-35	-21
	Δ(OIS rate)	-2	-7	-13	-20	-30	-31	-17	-11
	Δ(Yield-OIS spread)	-7	-11	-11	-16	-17	-10	-18	-10
6. August 12, 2009 (QE1)	Δ(US Treasury yield)	-3	-9	-12	-11	-10	-12	-3	0
	Δ(OIS rate)	-5	-8	-12	-14	-15	-13	-7	-5
	Δ(Yield-OIS spread)	2	-1	0	3	5	1	4	5
7. September 23, 2009 (QE1)	Δ(US Treasury yield)	-3	-9	-9	-8	-6	-6	-4	-3
	Δ(OIS rate)	-4	-9	-11	-11	-10	-10	-6	-5
	Δ(Yield-OIS spread)	1	0	2	3	4	4	2	2
8. November 4, 2009 (QE1)	Δ(US Treasury yield)	-2	-2	-2	-1	1	7	7	7
	Δ(OIS rate)	-4	-6	-5	-2	1	5	8	7
	Δ(Yield-OIS spread)	2	4	3	1	0	2	-1	0
9. August 10, 2010 (QE1)	Δ(US Treasury yield)	-1	0	-3	-10	-13	-14*	-11	-8
	Δ(OIS rate)	-2	-3	-6	-10	-16	-17	-16	-16
	Δ(Yield-OIS spread)	0	3	3	0	3	3	5	8

10. August 27, 2010 (QE2)								
Δ(US Treasury yield)	1	-1	-2	1	1	4	5	7
Δ(OIS rate)	0	0	3	3	0	-2	-8	-8
Δ(Yield-OIS spread)	1	-1	-5	-2	1	6	13	15
11. September 21, 2010 (QE2)								
Δ(US Treasury yield)	-1	-3	-5	-10	-14	-16**	-14	-13
Δ(OIS rate)	0	-3	-6	-9	-11	-13	-12	-15
Δ(Yield-OIS spread)	-1	0	1	-1	-3	-3	-2	2
12. November 3, 2010 (QE2)								
Δ(US Treasury yield)	-1	-1	-6	-11	-14	-10	4	11
Δ(OIS rate)	-1	-2	-6	-12	-11	-7	8	14
Δ(Yield-OIS spread)	1	1	0	1	-3	-3	-4	-3
13. September 21, 2011 (OT)								
Δ(US Treasury yield)	-2	2	4	-6	-15	-23***	-34	-42
Δ(OIS rate)	1	2	0	-10	-17	-26	-38	-43
Δ(Yield-OIS spread)	1	0	4	4	2	3	4	1
14. June 20, 2012 (OT)								
Δ(US Treasury yield)	0	2	2	2	1	-1	-3	-5
Δ(OIS rate)	1	2	3	3	2	1	-3	-4
Δ(Yield-OIS spread)	1	0	-1	-1	-1	-2	0	-1
15. August 22, 2012 (QE3)								
Δ(US Treasury yield)	0	-5	-6	-9	-12	-12	-12	-11
Δ(OIS rate)	-1	-3	-5	-8	-10	-11	-12	-11
Δ(Yield-OIS spread)	-1	-2	-1	-1	-2	-1	0	-1
16. September 13, 2012 (QE3)								
Δ(US Treasury yield)	0	2	2	2	6	11	16	17
Δ(OIS rate)	1	0	0	2	4	6	14	17
Δ(Yield-OIS spread)	-1	2	2	0	2	5	2	0
17. December 12, 2012 (QE3)								
Δ(US Treasury yield)	-2	3	2	6	9	8	8	7
Δ(OIS rate)	0	1	3	7	7	7	6	6
Δ(Yield-OIS spread)	-2	2	-1	-1	2	1	2	1
QE1-related events								
Δ(US Treasury yield)	-34	-64	-65	-104	-123	-132	-94	-77
Δ(OIS rate)	-34	-55	-77	-108	-124	-119	-75	-68
Δ(Yield-OIS spread)	0	-9	12	4	1	-13	-19	-9

(continued)

Table 4.5 (continued)

Event date	Change	1-year	2-year	3-year	5-year	7-year	10-year	20-year	30-year
QE2-related events	Δ(US Treasury yield)	-1	-5	-13	-20	-27	-22	-5	5
	Δ(OIS rate)	1	-5	-9	-18	-22	-21	-11	-10
	Δ(Yield-OIS spread)	-2	0	-4	-2	-5	-1	6	15
OT-related events	Δ(US Treasury yield)	2	4	6	-4	-14	-24	-37	-47
	Δ(OIS rate)	2	4	3	-7	-16	-25	-40	-46
	Δ(Yield-OIS spread)	0	0	3	3	2	1	3	-1
QE3-related events	Δ(US Treasury yield)	-3	0	-2	-1	3	7	12	13
	Δ(OIS rate)	-1	-2	-2	0	1	2	9	12
	Δ(Yield-OIS spread)	-2	2	0	-1	2	5	3	1
Total net change in the US Treasury yield		-36	-65	-74	-129	-161	-171	-124	-106
Total net change in USD OIS rate		-31	-58	-86	-132	-161	-163	-118	-112
Total net change in yield-OIS spread		-5	-7	12	3	0	-8	-6	6

Notes: All changes are measured in basis points. Cumulative changes may differ from the sum of changes reported for individual events because of rounding. QE1, QE2, and QE3 represent the first, second, and third rounds of quantitative easing, respectively; and OT represents operation twist. ***, **, and * indicate changes in interest rate outside the 0.5th and 99.5th percentile range, the 1st and 99th percentile range, and the 2.5th and 97.5th percentile range of the distribution of interest rate changes in normal time, respectively

According to the decomposition of interest rates specified in Sect. 4.1, the declines are likely to be driven by a shift in the expectations about the path of future short rates. Besides, yield-OIS spreads increase moderately at most of the maturities, and thus no evidence of portfolio rebalance effect is observed.

On December 1, 2008, Chairman Ben Bernanke indicates that the Fed could purchase a substantial quantity of long-term Treasuries or agency securities on the open market in an attempt to influence financial conditions and spur aggregate demand. The indication of purchasing long-term securities causes further declines in both Treasury yields and OIS rates which are significant across all maturities. However, the net changes in yield-OIS spreads are rather small. It is suggested that market participants revised their expectations about future policy rates downward after Chairman Ben Bernanke's speech.

The possible purchases of long-term Treasuries are mentioned for the first time in Federal Open Market Committee (FOMC) statement released on December 16, 2008. The Committee announces that the potential benefits of purchasing longer-term Treasury securities have been evaluated. As results, both Treasury yields and OIS rates further decline, and the declines are more pronounced for intermediate- and longer-term Treasuries with maturities over 5 years. The net changes in yield-OIS spreads are still relatively small, except that associated with 30-year Treasury bond.

After its meeting on January 28, 2009, the FOMC announces that the Federal Reserve is ready to expand its previously introduced agency debt and MBS purchases, and is prepared to initiate its longer-term Treasury securities purchases. Surprisingly, both Treasury yields and OIS rates rise significantly across all maturities around this announcement, suggesting that market participants raise their expectations about path of future short rates. The yield-OIS spreads, however, fall slightly at most maturities, which may reflect the limited QE effect through the portfolio rebalance channel.

The purchases of long-term Treasury securities are officially announced on March 18, 2009. The FOMC decides to purchase up to $300 billion of longer-term Treasury securities over the following 6 months. Meanwhile, the Committee decides to bring its maximum purchases of agency MBS from $500 billion to $1.25 trillion and of agency debt from $100 billion to $200 billion. Although the purchases of long-term Treasury securities have been well indicated in previous statements and have been widely expected by the market, Treasury yields fall sharply at all maturities after this announcement. The yields of longer- and intermediate-term Treasury bonds fall by up to 47 basis points. The OIS rates also fall but with smaller magnitudes, leading to significant declines in yield-spread rates across all maturities. The sharp decline in Treasury yields around the launch of long-term Treasury purchases, thus, reflects the combined effect of QE through both the signaling channel and portfolio rebalance channel.

In order to promote a smooth transition in markets, on August 12, 2009, the FOMC decides to gradually slow the pace of its large-scale asset purchases by setting the final purchases of Treasury securities at the end of October instead of mid-September 2009. This announcement is followed by further moderate drop in the Treasury yields and OIS rates, leaving the spreads between them roughly unchanged.

Similarly, the FOMC decides on September 23, 2009, to gradually slow the pace of agency debt and MBS purchases, by extending the purchase period to the first quarter of 2010. This announcement has similar effect to the previous one, leading to decline in both Treasury yields and IOS rates but marginal increase in the spreads. The slowdown in the pace of asset purchases may signal the Federal Reserve's commitment to keep the federal funds rate low for a longer period, and thus affect Treasure yields mainly through the signaling channel.

Given the limited availability of agency debt, the FOMC announces on November 4, 2009, that the amount of agency debt purchases would be capped at $175 billion instead of $200 billion as previously announced. This announcement does not cause significant change in interest rates. However, interest rates at different maturities react to the event differently. Both Treasury yields and OIS rates with shorter maturities fall marginally, while those with longer maturities rise slightly. The yield-OIS spreads remain roughly unchanged across all maturities.

In the statement released on August 10, 2010, the FOMC announces that it will keep constant the Federal Reserve's holdings of securities at their current level by reinvesting principal payments from agency debt and agency MBSs in longer-term Treasury securities.[9] The yields of medium- and longer-term bonds decline immediately after this announcement. Before this announcement, market participants widely expect that the Federal Reserve would let its MBS portfolio run off, influenced by Chairman Ben Bernanke mentioning the normalization of monetary policy earlier in his report to congress. This announcement therefore revises market expectations and signals that the focus of the unconventional monetary policy would shift toward longer-term Treasuries rather than agency debt or agency MBSs (Krishnamurthy and Vissing-Jorgensen 2011). OIS rates fall more sharply than their corresponding Treasury yields at almost all maturities, suggesting that the declines in Treasury yields are mainly due to lowered expectation toward future federal funds rate.

To sum up, our results show that the first round of unconventional monetary policy made by the Federal Reserve is effective in lowering the US Treasury yields, although agency debt and agency MBS account for more than 80 % of the assets purchased. Over the set of Fed's QE1-related events, the yields of the US Treasuries with maturities between 5 and 10 years decline significantly by over 120 basis points on average, while the yields of longer- and shorter-term US Treasuries also fall considerably by about 85 and 55 basis points, respectively. The US Treasury yield responses are mirrored in the OIS market. The fall in the OIS rates, which represent average expectations for the effective federal funds rate over their respective maturities, is quantitatively similar to the reaction pattern observed in the US

---

[9] Krishnamurthy and Vissing-Jorgensen (2011) offer a back-of-the-envelope calculation. Suppose that the repayment rate for the next year on the $1.1 trillions of MBSs is 20 % (the Federal Reserve's holding of MBSs is $1,118 billion on August 4, 2010), the FOMC statement implies that the Federal Reserve intends to purchase $220 billion ($1.1 trillion × 0.2) of Treasuries over the next year, $176 billion ($1.1 trillion × (1 − 0.2) × 0.2) over the subsequent year, and so on. However, in its meeting on September 21, 2011, the FOMC decides to reinvest maturing MBSs and agency debts in MBSs rather than Treasuries as previously announced in an attempt to support conditions in mortgage markets.

Treasury yields. The changes in the spreads between the US Treasury yields and their corresponding OIS rates, therefore, are hardly affected by the Fed's QE1-related announcements, indicating that the fall in the yields of the US Treasuries is largely attributable to the shift in the expectations about future short interest rates. The robustness check results reported in Appendix B yield similar conclusions, and are largely consistent with those offered by Christensen and Rudebusch (2012) who also use a 1-day event window.

4.5.1.3 Fed's QE2-Related Events (Events 10–12)

Given the worrisome deflation trend in 2010, the Fed begins to signal that more asset purchases are likely to be undertaken. In a speech on August 27, 2010, Chairman Ben Bernanke indicates that further monetary ease policy options are available and will certainly be used to maintain price stability and provide additional stimulus, should further action prove necessary. This speech, however, does not cause significant reactions in bond and OIS markets, which might be because the second round of QE has been widely expected even before the speech given the bad economic news released in early 2010.[10]

The Fed's intention to maintain the policy of reinvesting principal payments from its securities holdings is repeated in its FOMC statement on September 21, 2010. The repetition of the intention leads to further drop in both Treasury yields and OIS rates, especially for those with maturities over 5 years. Krishnamurthy and Vissing-Jorgensen (2011) argue that the market reactions are likely to be attributable to the new language used in this announcement which can be read as indicating new stimulus by the Fed and particularly an expansion of its purchases of longer-term Treasuries.

The second round of QE is finally announced after the FOMC meeting on November 3, 2010. The Committee decides to purchase a further $600 billion of longer-term Treasury securities at a pace of about $75 billion per month, which is explicitly designed to lower longer-term interest rates. Since the expansion of the Treasury securities purchases has been widely expected by market participants and been largely reflected in asset prices, this announcement has relatively limited impact on interest rates. In fact, a survey of private sector economists conducted by the *Wall Street Journal* in early October 2010 shows that they expect the Federal Reserve to purchase about $750 billion in QE2. The FOMC's actual decision of $600 billion purchase is, thus, somewhat below the market expectation (Krishnamurthy and Vissing-Jorgensen 2011). As a result, both Treasury yields and OIS rates at longer maturities above 10 years rise moderately around this announcement.

The effects of the Fed's QE2 on interest rates are consistently much smaller than those found for its QE1 across the yield curve. The yields of medium-term US Treasuries with maturities between 5 and 10 years fall but only by about 20 basis

---

[10] Krishnamurthy and Vissing-Jorgensen (2011) assert that the market may update its perception of QE2 not only on Federal Reserve's announcement dates but also on dates of bad economic news.

points over the set of QE2-related events, while those associated with longer- and shorter-term Treasuries are even less. Our findings are consistent with the results offered by Krishnamurthy and Vissing-Jorgensen (2011) who find no dramatic Treasury yield declines right around the QE2-related events even if intraday Treasury yield data is used. Besides, our results also suggest that, like QE1, the limited effect of QE2 on interest rates works primarily through the signaling channel, as there is no significant decline in the spreads between Treasury yields and their corresponding OIS rates. The 1-day changes in interest rates around the set of QE2-related events, as presented in Appendix B, show that the Fed's QE2 fails to lower longer-term interest rates at all maturities. Instead, longer-term interest rates increase by more than 20 basis points.

4.5.1.4   Fed's OT-Related Events (Events 13–14)

Economic indicators released in the summer of 2011 point to continuing weakness in economic growth and labor market conditions. In response, the Fed decides to extend the average maturity of its holdings of securities by purchasing $400 billion of Treasury securities with remaining maturities of 6–30 years and simultaneously selling an equal amount of Treasury securities with remaining maturities of 3 years or less. The so-called operation twist (OT) aims to put downward pressures on longer-term interest rates and reduce their spreads with respect to shorter-term interest rates. Although the operation twist does not expand the monetary base, the announcement successfully brings down longer-term interest rates.[11] The yields of 20- and 30-year US Treasuries drop substantially by 34 and 42 basis points, respectively. The yields of medium-term Treasuries with maturities between 5 and 10 years also fall noticeably around the announcement of OT. Decomposing the changes in Treasury yields suggests that the declines in longer-term interest rates are mainly attributable to the lowering expectation about future short rates rather than the decreases in term premium.

In an attempt to make the broader financial conditions more accommodative, the Fed decides to extend its operation twist program by adding additionally purchases and sales of $267 billion and thereby extending the program throughout 2012. The extension of OT, however, is not as effective as the initial announcement of the program in terms of bringing down longer-term interest rates. Both Treasury yields and OIS rates remain roughly unchanged around the release of the news. Overall, the Fed's OT-related events lower longer- and medium-term Treasury yields by about 40 and 20 basis points, respectively, without significantly raising shorter-term Treasury yields. The main transmission mechanism by which OT program works through is still the signaling channel. No evidence of portfolio rebalance effect is observed.

---

[11] The longer-term Treasury securities purchased are funded by shorter-term Treasury securities sold, and therefore there is no money creation.

4.5.1.5   Fed's QE3-Related Events (Events 15–17)

Despite the previous efforts, the unemployment rate remains elevated. Many FOMC members expect that the unemployment rate would still be well above their estimates of its longer-term normal rate. They, therefore, indicate in the FOMC minutes that additional monetary accommodation would likely be warranted fairly soon to improve the labor market conditions. The release of the FOMC minutes on August 22, 2012, is followed by a moderate fall by about 10 basis points in the yields of longer- and medium-term Treasuries. The same pattern is also observed in the OIS rates, and thus leaves the yield-OIS spreads across all maturities approximately unchanged.

After its meeting on September 13, 2012, the FOMC announces a new $40 billion a month purchasing program of agency MBSs. The program is open-ended, which means that it would continue in the context of price stability until the labor market improves substantially. Since the additional monetary accommodation has been widely expected, the actual announcement of QE3 does not lead to further decline in interest rates. In fact, the US Treasury yields as well as OIS rates increase at almost all maturities around this announcement.

To further support progress toward maximum employment and price stability, the FOMC decides to continue purchase longer-term Treasury securities at a pace of $45 billion per month after completing its OT program at the end of 2012. Like the purchases of MBSs previously announced, the $45 billion worth longer-term Treasury securities purchases would continue until the economic recovery strengthens. Therefore, the Federal Reserve would purchase $85 billion worth assets every month for a considerable time under QE3. Despite the large amount of asset to be purchased, the announcement of QE3 does not reduce Treasury yields effectively. The longer-term Treasury yields as well as their corresponding OIS rates cumulatively rise slightly over the set of QE3-related events, which is surprising given the main objective of the program is to depress long-term yields to stimulate the economy.

4.5.1.6   Cumulative Changes Over Fed's QE-Related Events (Events 1–17)

Overall, our empirical results show that the Fed's unconventional monetary policies are effective in lowering interest rates, particularly for those associated at medium and longer maturities. On average, the yields of Treasuries with maturities over 5 years drop by about 140 basis points, while the yields of Treasuries with shorter maturities also fall considerably by about 60 basis points. The decomposition of interest rate suggests that almost the entire decline in the US Treasury yields is attributable to decrease in OIS rates, implying that the Fed's unconventional monetary policies are particularly effective in lowering expectations of future short rates through the signaling channel. The portfolio rebalance channel, however, is not operative as indicated by the relatively unchanged yield-IOS spreads over the set of QE-related events. These findings are largely consistent with those of Christensen and Rudebusch (2012) who examine the first round of QE in the USA and the UK. More importantly, our results provide additional evidence to highlight the importance of the signaling channel in the Fed's unconventional monetary policy measures, not only the APPs but also the operation twist program.

In addition, our results reveal new insight that the effectiveness of QE in the USA diminishes over time. More specifically, the limited effect of QE2 and QE3 is in sharp contrast to the significant impact of QE1 in terms of bringing down interest rates across the entire yield curve. Take 10-year constant maturity Treasury yield for example; it drops cumulatively by about 130 basis points over the events related to the first round of QE. By contrast, it falls by only about 20 basis points around the set of QE2-related announcements, and it rises slightly around the set of QE3-related announcements. On average, more than 80 % of the cumulative decline in Treasury yields is attributable to the first round of QE, while the subsequent unconventional monetary policies only contribute less than 20 % to the cumulative change in interest rates. Therefore, the unconventional monetary policy measures undertaken by the Fed are losing steam.

Besides, the 1-day changes in the US Treasury yields, OIS rates, and yields-OIS spreads around the set of QE-related events reported in Appendix B are consistently much smaller than their 2-day counterparts. Our results lend empirical support to the argument by Krishnamurthy and Vissing-Jorgensen (2011) that, given the relative novelty of the large-scale asset purchases and the diversity of beliefs about the mechanisms by which they operate, changes have been absorbed more slowly than for typical monetary policy shocks such as those to the policy rate. Therefore, the 2-day event window is likely to be more appropriate to assess the effect of the unconventional monetary policies such as QE and OT. The differences between 2- and 1-day changes in interest rates are particularly large on the long end of the yield curve, which suggests that it takes longer time for the unconventional measures to affect the price and thus the yield of low-liquidity assets.

4.5.2 Evidence from the UK

4.5.2.1 UK Gilt Yields (November 1, 2008–December 31, 2012)

Figure 4.2 depicts the movements in the yields of UK government securities (gilts) with different maturities over the period from November 2008 to the end of 2012. The vertical lines represent the Bank of England's QE-related announcements as listed in our event set for the UK. It shows that the most significant declines in UK gilt yields occur around the first two pieces of QE-related news released by the BOE on February 11 and March 5, 2009, respectively. Moderate decreases in UK gilt yields are also observed right after the Monetary Policy Committee (MPC) meetings held in May, August, and November 2009, and those in February and July 2012. Overall, comparing their levels at the end of 2012 to those before the start of QE in 2008 suggests that UK gilt yields reduce evidently at all maturities. To more carefully examine the direct impact of the BOE's unconventional monetary policies, we focus on the UK market reactions over a 2-day event window around each of the QE-related announcements listed in Table 4.2.

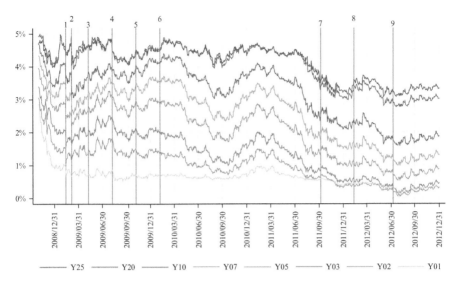

Fig. 4.2 UK gilt yields at different maturities. *Sources*: UK government liability nominal spot yield curves are obtained from the Bank of England. *Note*: *Vertical lines* represent the BOE's QE-related events listed in Table 4.2

4.5.2.2 BOE's QE1-Related Events (Events 1–6)

Table 4.6 reports 2-day changes in UK gilt yields, OIS rates, and yield-OIS spreads at different maturities around the Bank of England's QE-related announcements. It clearly shows that UK gilt yields fall significantly at all maturities after the release of the first piece of QE-related news on February 11, 2009. The BOE's *Inflation Report* published and the associated press conference held on that day give a strong indication that unconventional monetary policy is likely to be undertaken to increase the supply of money, which in turn is expected to stimulate nominal spending and keeps inflation at its 2 % target.[12] As a consequence, UK gilt yields fall substantially at all maturities right around this event. The response is most pronounced for shorter- and medium-term (up to 10 years) gilts whose yields fall by over 30 basis points, while the reaction on the long end of the yield curve (above 10 years) is relatively weak. The asymmetric responses across the yield curve may suggest that the market initially perceives that the BOE would target purchases on shorter-maturity gilts (see Joyce et al. 2011a, b). Meanwhile, the OIS rates based on GBP also drop noticeably around this event, ranging from 2 to 28 basis points. The declined OIS rates reflect lowered market expectations about future policy rate after the publication of *Inflation Report* and the associated press conference.[13] The resulting decrease

---

[12] See the BOE's February Inflation Report (2009) and the press conference transcript via: http://www.bankofengland.co.uk/publications/Pages/inflationreport/ir0901.aspx

[13] Joyce et al. (2011a, b) suggest that the publication of the February Inflation Report is also associated with an increased expectation that Bank Rate would be cut to 0.5 % in March.

Table 4.6 Two-day changes in UK gilt yields, OIS rates, and yield-OIS spreads

Event date	Change	1-year	2-year	3-year	5-year	7-year	10-year	15-year	20-year	25-year
1. February 11, 2009 (QE1)	Δ(UK gilt yield)	-30	-44	-44	-41	-38	-35***	-24	-15	-13
	Δ(OIS rate)	-24	-28	-26	-24	-22	-20	-12	-5	-2
	Δ(Yield-OIS spread)	-6	-16	-18	-17	-16	-15	-12	-10	-11
2. March 5, 2009 (QE1)	Δ(UK gilt yield)	5	2	-7	-34	-55	-68***	-83	-89	-76
	Δ(OIS rate)	21	12	2	-9	-17	-26	-33	-34	-25
	Δ(Yield-OIS spread)	-16	-10	-9	-25	-38	-42	-50	-55	-51
3. May 7, 2009 (QE1)	Δ(UK gilt yield)	1	6	8	8	9	10*	5	1	3
	Δ(OIS rate)	1	5	10	18	20	20	20	17	14
	Δ(Yield-OIS spread)	0	1	-2	-10	-11	-10	-15	-16	-11
4. August 6, 2009 (QE1)	Δ(UK gilt yield)	0	0	-3	-4	-2	-3	-15	-26	-28
	Δ(OIS rate)	-4	-2	1	6	9	9	7	6	4
	Δ(Yield-OIS spread)	4	2	-4	-10	-11	-12	-22	-32	-32
5. November 5, 2009 (QE1)	Δ(UK gilt yield)	-3	-4	-2	4	8	10*	8	6	3
	Δ(OIS rate)	-5	-5	-3	2	5	9	9	7	5
	Δ(Yield-OIS spread)	2	1	1	2	3	1	-1	-1	-2
6. February 4, 2010 (QE1)	Δ(UK gilt yield)	-2	-4	-5	-4	-4	-2	-1	0	0
	Δ(OIS rate)	-5	-15	-14	-12	-12	-8	-6	-5	-5
	Δ(Yield-OIS spread)	3	11	9	8	8	6	5	5	5
7. October 6, 2011 (QE2)	Δ(UK gilt yield)	2	4	5	7	11	12**	5	1	-1
	Δ(OIS rate)	4	11	12	13	13	13	10	7	4
	Δ(Yield-OIS spread)	-2	-7	-7	-6	-2	-1	-5	-6	-5
8. February 9, 2012 (QE2)	Δ(UK gilt yield)	0	-4	-8	-12	-12	-5	6	12	12
	Δ(OIS rate)	-1	-2	-4	-5	-2	-1	3	5	7
	Δ(Yield-OIS spread)	1	-2	-4	-7	-10	-4	3	7	5
9. July 5, 2012 (QE3)	Δ(UK gilt yield)	-3	-9	-12	-14	-13	-11**	-8	-6	-3
	Δ(OIS rate)	-2	-3	-5	-9	-12	-11	-10	-9	-7
	Δ(Yield-OIS spread)	-1	-6	-7	-5	-1	0	2	3	4

QE1-related events	Δ(UK gilt yield)	−29	−44	−53	−71	−82	−88	−110	−123	−111
	Δ(OIS rate)	−15	−35	−32	−18	−17	−16	−15	−14	−8
	Δ(Yield-OIS spread)	−14	−9	−21	−53	−65	−72	−95	−109	−103
QE2-related events	Δ(UK gilt yield)	2	0	−3	−5	−1	7	11	13	11
	Δ(OIS rate)	4	9	8	8	11	11	13	13	10
	Δ(Yield-OIS spread)	−2	−9	−11	−13	−12	−4	−2	1	1
QE3-related events	Δ(UK gilt yield)	−3	−9	−12	−14	−13	−11	−8	−6	−3
	Δ(OIS rate)	−2	−3	−5	−9	−12	−11	−10	−9	−7
	Δ(Yield-OIS spread)	−1	−6	−7	−5	−1	0	2	3	4
Total net change in UK gilt yield		−30	−53	−68	−90	−96	−92	−107	−116	−103
Total net change in GBP OIS rate		−13	−29	−29	−20	−18	−16	−12	−10	−4
Total net change in yield-OIS spread		−17	−24	−39	−70	−78	−76	−95	−106	−99

Notes: All changes are measured in basis points. Cumulative changes may differ from the sum of changes reported for individual events because of rounding. QE1, QE2, and QE3 represent the first, second, and third rounds of quantitative easing, respectively. ***, **, and * indicate changes in interest rate outside the 0.5th and 99.5th percentile range, the 1st and 99th percentile range, and the 2.5th and 97.5th percentile range of the distribution of interest rate changes in normal time, respectively

in UK gilt yield-OIS spreads captures the impact of QE on gilt yields through port-folio rebalance channel. The fall in UK gilt yields around this event, therefore, rep-resents a combined effect of QE on interest rate through both the signaling and portfolio rebalance channels.

After some initial hesitations in adopting unconventional measures, the MPC of the BOE announces its APP on March 5, 2009, under which £75 billion of assets would be purchased over 3 months by issuing central bank reserves. As previously indicated, the objective of the program is to boost money supply through large-scale asset purchases which in turn is expected to raise the rate of growth of nominal spending to a level consistent with meeting the inflation target in the medium term. The UK gilt purchases, which are likely to be the majority of the overall purchases, are set to be restricted to medium- and long-term bonds. This announcement lowers gilt yields with maturities above 5 years dramatically by as much as 89 basis points. In contrast, gilt yields at shorter maturities increase only slightly around the announcement. A similar pattern is observed in OIS rates, but the fall on the long end is much smaller than that registered in comparable gilt yields. These reactions may imply that market participants revise their initial expectations that the asset purchases would focus on shorter-maturity gilts. The yield-OIS spreads fall signifi-cantly across all maturities, with those at longer maturities declining by up to 55 basis points, while those at shorter maturities fall much less. The decomposition of market responses, therefore, suggests that the commencement of the first round of QE not only lowers the expected future interest rates in the long run through the signaling channel but also reduces term premium of gilt yields across the entire yield curve through the portfolio rebalance channel. It is worth noting that the launch of the APP is announced alongside the Bank Rate cut, and thus the changes in gilt yields and OIS rates may not be entirely attributable to QE.[14]

After its meeting on May 7, 2009, the MPC announces the first extension of its APP by £50 billion to a total of £125 billion (over another 3 months). Compared with the first two events, this announcement has relatively limited impact on interest rates. Both gilt yields and OIS rates rise at all maturities around this event. Since the rises in OIS rates are relatively more noticeable, the yield-OIS spreads decline fur-ther at medium- and long-maturities by about 10–15 basis points. Joyce et al. (2011a, b) assert that this event has limited effect on interest rates because the exten-sion of QE has been widely anticipated by the market before the announcement.

The amount of the BOE's QE asset purchases is extended by a further £50 billion to a total of £175 billion on August 6, 2009. Meanwhile, the range of UK gilts eli-gible for purchases is also expanded to include all conventional gilts with a mini-mum residual maturity of greater than 3 years. Although the increase in the size of the APP has been widely expected, the expansion of buying range leads to further fall in gilt yields and yield-OIS spreads at medium and longer maturities. In con-trast, the gilt yields at 1- and 2-year maturities, which are outside the purchase range, remain unchanged around the event, and their corresponding yield-OIS

---

[14] Joyce et al. (2011a, b) argue that the Bank Rate cut has been widely expected and any resulting reactions are likely to have been confined to the short end of the curve.

spreads increase by a small amount. This finding provides additional evidence that the BOE's QE impacts gilt yields mainly through the portfolio rebalance channel.

On November 5, 2009, the BOE decides to expand its QE APP by another £25 billion to a total of £200 billion. Both gilt yields and OIS rates fall slightly at shorter maturities (less than 5 years), but increase moderately at medium and longer maturities (over 5 years). The movements in gilt yields and OIS rates around this event are likely to be driven by a common factor, which leaves the yield-OIS spreads at all maturities roughly unchanged.

On February 4, 2010, the MPC decides to maintain its QE program at £200 billion. The pause in asset purchases does not affect UK gilt yields significantly. However, OIS rates drop across all maturities around the announcement. The spreads between gilt yields and their corresponding OIS rates, therefore, increase up to about 10 basis points. Although Joyce et al. (2011a, b) argue that this decision has been widely anticipated and thus contains little news for asset prices, our results show that the pause in purchasing gilts may result in rise in gilt-specific premiums through the portfolio rebalance channel.

In summary, the first-round QE conducted by the BOE is proven to be effective in lowering UK gilt yields. The yields of UK gilts at longer maturities (above 10 years) fall significantly by more than 100 basis points over the set of QE1-related events. Those associated with medium (between 5 and 10) and shorter (below 5 years) maturities also drop considerably by about 80 and 40 basis points, respectively. Unlike in the QE conducted by the US Federal Reserve, the portfolio rebalance channel plays a much more important role in the BOE's QE. Over 80 % of the drop in the longer- and medium-term gilt yields around the set of QE1-related events is attributable to the net changes in their corresponding yield-OIS spreads through the portfolio rebalance channel, while the decline in shorter-term gilt yields represents a combined effect of QE on interest rates through both the signaling and portfolio rebalance channels.

4.5.2.3 BOE's QE2-Related Events (Events 7–8)

The deterioration in economic outlook in 2011 makes it more likely that inflation will undershoot the 2 % target in the medium term. After its meeting on October 6, 2011, the MPC announces the resumption of its QE program. The BOE decides to extend its APP to a total of £275 billion. The range of eligible gilts remains unchanged for this round of asset purchases, and thus includes all conventional gilts with a residual maturity greater than 3 years. However, UK gilt yields rise marginally at almost all maturities after this announcement. OIS rates also rise simultaneously, with slightly large magnitudes. The decision to resume QE asset purchases thus leads to further drop in yield-OIS spread. Market response to this event is much less significant compared with that associated with the initial announcement of the BOE's QE1 in 2009.

On February 9, 2012, the MPC votes to increase the size of its QE asset purchases by another £50 billion to a total of £325 billion. This announcement has mixed effects on gilt yields and OIS rates across maturities. While both gilt yields and OIS rates at shorter and medium maturities fall around this event, those at longer maturities rise. Meanwhile, yield-OIS spreads also fall at shorter and medium maturities, and rise at longer maturities. Overall, the second round of BOE's QE fails to further bring down interest rates in the UK. In fact, UK gilt yields at longer maturities increase moderately over the BOE's QE2-related events. This is in sharp contrast to the significant declines observed around the set of QE1-related events.

4.5.2.4   BOE's QE3-Related Event (Event 9)

Concerned with the continuation of the economic weakness both at home and abroad, the BOE announces the most recent extension of its QE APP after the MPC meeting held on July 5, 2012. The purchase of further £50 billion of assets takes the total size of the program to £375 billion. Both gilt yields and OIS rates fall moderately at all maturities around this event. The yield-OIS spreads, therefore, do not change much, falling marginally at shorter and medium maturities and rising slightly at longer maturities. It seems that the BOE's QE3 impacts gilt yields mainly through the signaling channel. The relative importance of the portfolio rebalance channel appears to decrease in the UK over time.

4.5.2.5   Cumulative Changes Over BOE's QE-Related Events (Events 1–9)

Over the entire set of events related to the BOE's QE program, the results reported in Table 4.6 show that longer-term (above 10 years) UK gilt yields fall significantly by about 110 basis points; medium-term (between 5 and 10 years) gilt yields fall about 90 basis points; and shorter-term (below 5 years) gilt yields fall much less, by about 50 basis points. The cumulative decline in OIS rates over the same set of events is much smaller, by around 25, 20, and 10 basis points at shorter, medium, and longer maturities, respectively. Decomposing the changes in gilt yields suggests that the fall in gilt yields is largely attributable to the decline in yield-OIS spreads. More precisely, about 90 % of the cumulative declines in longer-term UK gilt yields are attributable to the changes in their corresponding yield-OIS rates, about 80 % for those at medium term, and about 50 % for those at shorter term. Our empirical evidence, therefore, suggests that the BOE's QE asset purchases impact interest rates mainly through the portfolio rebalance effect, while the policy expectation channel plays a much less important role in affecting gilt yields in the UK. This finding is consistent with previous studies on the first round of QE in the UK, such as Joyce et al. (2011a, b) and Christensen and Rudebusch (2012). In addition, our results also show that the portfolio rebalance effect evidenced in the first round of QE becomes less obvious in the second and third rounds of QE conducted by the BOE, while the signaling effect begins to play an important role in explaining the interest rate responses around BOE's QE2- and QE3-related events, at least on the long end of the yield curve.

Our results also show that, like in the USA, the unconventional monetary measures implemented in the UK become less effective in lowering interest rates over the past 4 years. Over 80 % of the cumulative changes in gilt yields and over 70 % of the cumulative changes in yield-OIS rates are attributable to the set of QE1-related events observed in 2009 and 2010. Compared with the first round of QE, the BOE's second and third rounds of QE announced in 2011 and 2012 have limited impacts on interest rates. In fact, both gilt yields and yield-OIS spreads increase slightly at longer maturities over the BOE's QE2- and QE3-related events. It seems that the effectiveness of the BOE's QE also diminishes over time. However, it is possible to argue that the diminishing effect of QE observed in our event study may reflect the fact that the market has already priced in much of the expected impact before the second and third rounds of QE are announced given the bad economic news released.

To determine the robustness of our empirical results presented in this section, 1-day changes in UK gilt yields, OIS rates, and yield-OIS spreads at different maturities around the BOE's QE-related announcements are reported in Appendix C. It shows the absolute 1-day changes in UK gilt yields and yield-OIS are almost always significantly smaller than their 2-day counterparts, which implies that it takes relatively longer time for the unconventional monetary policies to be fully reflected in the UK market. Overall, the main conclusions in this section remain valid even if a 1-day event window is used.

4.5.3   Evidence from Japan

4.5.3.1   Japan Government Bond Yields (November 1, 2008–February 28, 2013)

Figure 4.3 depicts the movements in the yields of Japanese government bonds (JGBs) at different maturities over the period from November 2008 to the end of 2012. The vertical lines represent the large set of BOJ's QE-related events listed in Table 4.3. It is evident that the unconventional monetary policy of the BOJ is characterized by a series of regular policy changes, which is different from that of the US Fed's "big bang" approach.[15] Comparing to Figs. 4.1, 4.2, and 4.4, Fig. 4.3 shows that the interest rate levels in Japan are much lower than those observed in the other major advanced economies, such as the USA, the UK, and euro area, throughout the whole period under investigation. This is attributable mainly to the so-called zero interest rate policy (ZIRP) introduced in 1999 by the BOJ as the core of its monetary policy to cope with deteriorating economic conditions and deflation risk. Although the ZIRP is abandoned in 2006 in light of the favorable developments in economic conditions and the reduced deflation pressures, the low level of the policy rate is maintained in Japan. Although JGB yields fall across all maturities over the

---

[15] The US Fed typically monitors its unconventional monetary policy measures for at least half a year, and undertakes another big stimulus if it is necessary.

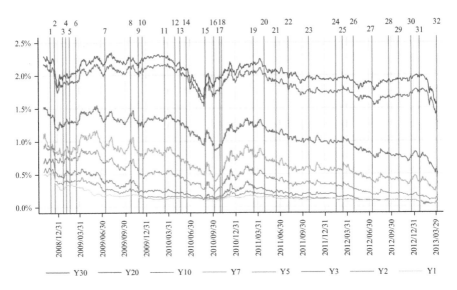

Fig. 4.3 Japanese government bond yields at different maturities. *Sources*: Japanese government bond yields are obtained from Ministry of Finance Japan. *Note*: *Vertical lines* represent the BOJ's QE-related events listed in Table **4.3**

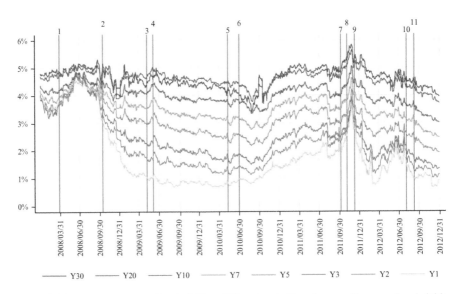

Fig. 4.4 Euro area government bond yields at different maturities. *Sources*: Euro area bond yields are obtained from the European Central Bank. *Note*: *Vertical lines* represent the ECB's QE-related events listed in Table 4.4

QE period, the decline in government bond yields in Japan is not of the same magnitude as those observed in the USA and the UK. To precisely assess the effectiveness of the Bank of Japan's unconventional monetary policies, we focus on the fairly narrow window around each of the BOJ's QE-related event dates.

4.5.3.2 BOJ's SFSO-Related Events (Events 1, 5, 7, and 8)

In response to the recent global economic crisis, the BOJ's QE starts with the SFSOs announced on December 2, 2008, right after the commencement of the US Fed's large-scale APP. Through the SFSOs, the BOJ offers unlimited amount of loans with maturities less than 3 months against the value of corporate debt pledged as the standing pool of eligible collateral to banks over the fiscal year-end at an interest rate equivalent to the target for the uncollateralized overnight call rate which is 0.3 %. Since the BOJ cut its policy rate on December 19, 2008, the interest rate applied to the SFSOs further reduces to 0.1 %. Although the introduction of the program does not see sharp increase in the central bank's balance sheet in 2008 (Fawley and Neely 2013), its initial announcement slightly lowers the yields of JGB at almost all maturities by around three basis points.

The SFSO program is subsequently extended three times in 2009 and then is set to expire in March 2010. However, all these SFSO-related announcements are made by the BOJ's Policy Board alongside some other policy decisions. It is, therefore, difficult to isolate their impact on interest rates. The first expansion of the SFSO is announced on February 19, 2009, with a view to facilitating a decline in longer-term interest rates. The Policy Board expands the program by increasing its frequency (from twice a month to once a week), extending the duration of each loan (from within 3 months to 3 months), and extending the operations through the end of September 2009. The period for which the operations remain in effect is further extended on July 15, 2009, to the end of calendar year, and again on October 30, 2009, to the end of the fiscal year. The subsequent extensions of the program, however, are not effective in facilitating decline in interest rates. Although JGB yields fall slightly at the long end of the curve around October 30, 2009, the decline is more likely to be attributable to the introduction of the new fixed-rate funds-supplying operations (FRFSO) by the BOJ on the same day.

To sum up, JGB yields fall slightly across all maturities with an average of three basis points over the set of SFSO-related events. Unlike in the USA and the UK, the difference between 1- and 2-day changes in government bond yields in Japan is not significant (see Appendix D), which suggests that the Japanese market responds to the central bank's unconventional monetary policy more promptly. Since the OIS rates based on JPY are not available at most of the maturities before the end of 2009, we are not able to disentangle the channels through which the SFSOs impact interest rates.

4.5.3.3 BOJ's OAP-Related Events (Events 2–7)

In addition to cut policy rate from around 0.3 to around 0.1 % on December 19, 2008, the BOJ also decides to increase its OAPs. Purchases of JGBs are increased for the first time since 2002 from ¥14.4 trillion to ¥16.8 trillion per year. The central bank also hits at the possible outright purchases of corporate finance instruments. The increase in OAPs lowers JGB yields at all maturities, with an average of seven basis points. On March 18, 2009, another increase in annual purchase of JGBs from ¥16.8 trillion to ¥21.6 trillion leads to further falls in interest rates, especially for those at medium maturities.

Following up the announcement made on December 19, 2008, the outright purchases of commercial paper up to ¥3 trillion, stock held by financial institutions up to ¥1 trillion, and corporate bonds up to ¥1 trillion are revealed by the BOJ on January 22, February 3, 2009, and February 19, 2009, respectively. In order to continue facilitating corporate finance and ensuring market stability, the periods for which these temporary measures operate are extended simultaneously on July 15, 2009. These announcements with respect to the outright purchases of corporate finance instruments may contribute to the improvement in market liquidity, but are not effective in lowering interest rates.

On average, JGB yields at shorter and medium maturities fall cumulatively by seven basis points over the set of OAP-related events, while those at longer maturities rise marginally. The robustness check results reported in Appendix D show that the 1-day decline in JGB yields at shorter and medium maturities around the set of OAP-related events represents only about half of the decline registered in their 2-day counterparts. This suggests that it takes relatively longer time for the effect of the OAPs to be transmitted into asset prices and yields. However, in the absence of OIS rates at most of the maturities, the transmission mechanism through which the interest rates are affected by the OAP-related events cannot be identified.

4.5.3.4 BOJ's FRO-Related Events (Events 8, 9, 11, and 15)

On October 30, 2009, the BOJ gives an indication that the existing SFSOs would be replaced with new FROs from April 2010, to further encourage decline in longer-term interest rate by providing ample liquidity. Although the total amount of loans to be provided is fixed, a wider range of collateral will be accepted under the new operations. A total amount of ¥10 trillion 3-month loans at a fixed target interest rate of 0.1 % is officially announced on December 1, 2009. The launch of the FROs indeed brings down both JGB yields and OIS rates significantly across all maturities. The yield-OIS spreads remain relatively unchanged, which indicates that the launch of FROs reduces interest rates mainly by lowering the markets expectation about future short rates through the signaling channel.

Given the decline in the amount of outstanding SFSOs, the BOJ decides, on March 17, 2010, to double the total amount of its 3-month FROs to ¥20 trillion. The expansion of FROs, however, does not further reduce interest rates. Instead, JGB yields at medium maturities rise slightly within the 2-day event window. On August 30, 2010, 6-month FROs up to of ¥10 trillion are introduced by the central bank. The total amount of loans under FROs, thus, reaches ¥30 trillion. The introduction of 6-month FROs is followed by slight declines in both JGB yields and OIS rates by about three basis points, implying that the longer-term FROs to some extent lower market perception about future interest rates.

Our empirical results, therefore, show that the set of FRO-related events are moderately effective in encouraging decline in interest rates. JGB yields decline at all maturities, on average, by about ten basis points. OIS rates also fall across the curve but with smaller sizes. The spreads between JGB yields and their corresponding OIS rates remain relatively unchanged except those at longer maturities. Thus, empirical evidence from Japan suggests that the FRO-related events affect shorter- and medium-term interest rates mainly through the signaling channel, but impact longer-term interest rate chiefly via the portfolio rebalance channel.

4.5.3.5 BOJ's GSFF-Related Events (Events 12–14, 21, and 25)

Given the critical challenge of overcoming deflation and strengthening economic growth, the BOJ's Policy Board indicates, after its meeting on April 30, 2010, that new efforts would be made to support private financial institutions in terms of fund provisioning. Following the initial indication, the preliminary framework for the fund-provisioning measure to facilitate strengthening of the foundations for economic growth is released on May 21, 2010. The duration of the loans to be provided under this measure is set to 1 year. On June 15, 2010, the GSFF is formally announced. The central bank decides to provide a total amount of ¥3 trillion in 1-year loans through the GSFF. Each loan is allowed to be rolled over up to three times, and thus has a maximum duration of 4 years. On June 14, 2011, additional ¥500 billion in loans are made available to private financial institutions for equity investment and asset-based lending. On March 13, 2012, another ¥2 trillion in loans are made available, taking the maximum amount of funds available under this facility to ¥5.5 trillion.

Interest rates across the curve respond to the introduction and subsequent extensions of the GSFF differently. Specifically, JGB yields at longer maturities fall by about five basis points, while those at medium maturities rise by about six basis points. Interest rates at shorter maturities are not affected by the GSFF-related events. The mixed impact of GSFF-related events on interest rates across the yield curve makes it more difficult to disentangle the channels through which the JGB yields are affected. It seems that the decline in longer-term JGB yields is more likely to be attributable to the portfolio rebalance effect induced by the GSFF-related events.

4.5.3.6 BOJ's CME-Related Events (Events 16–19, 22–24, and 26–31)

In response to the slowing down in economic recovery in late 2010, the BOJ introduces its CME policy on October 5. The CME is composed of three measures. First, the targeted policy rate is lowered from around 0.1 to around 0–0.1 %, i.e., a virtually ZIRP. Second, the virtually ZIRP would be maintained in effect until the monetary authority judges that price stability is in sight. Third, an APP is established to purchase various financial assets, including Japanese government securities, commercial paper, corporate bonds, exchange-traded funds (ETFs), as well as Japanese real estate investment trusts (J-REIT), and to conduct the existing FROs. The size of the program is expected to be about ¥35 trillion which includes about ¥30 trillion under the existing FROs. It is also indicated that government securities are likely to form the majority of the ¥5 trillion newly introduced asset purchases. The operational details of the APP are released after the subsequent Policy Board meetings held on October 28, 2010, and November 5, 2010. Despite the efforts made by the BOJ, significant decline in JGB yields is observed only for those at medium maturities around the initial introduction of the CME on October 5, 2010. As indicated by the changes in OIS rates, the limited impact of the CME on JGB yields is likely to be transmitted through the signaling channel by lowering market expectation about future short rates.

From March 2011 to the end of 2012, the size of asset purchases under the program is incrementally expanded nine times from about ¥5 trillion to about ¥76 trillion, while the size of the fixed-rate fund-supplying operations reduces by about ¥5 trillion from ¥30 trillion to ¥25 trillion. The total size of the APP, thus, reaches ¥101 trillion by the end of 2012. As can be seen from Table 4.7, most of the announcements regarding the expansion of the APP are followed by decline in interest rates; however, no significant change is observed. Noticeable decline in OIS rates is only observed around the first expansion announced on March 14, 2011. Our empirical evidence, therefore, suggests that constant and frequent tinkering with settings of the policy measures is not an effective way to encourage decline in interest rates in Japanese market.

At the end of 2012, Mr. Shinzo Abe takes office as the new Prime Minister of Japan. He urges the BOJ to take more decisive and effective policy steps to stem the continuous price decline and the sluggish private investment and spending which are generally regarded as the causes of the stagnant Japanese economy over the last 2 decades. His plan which combines aggressive central bank easing as well as large government spending is dubbed "Abenomics." Under the pressure from the new government, the BOJ decides to provide additional monetary accommodation by setting a higher price stability target and extending its APP indefinitely.[16] More specifically, the price stability target is set at 2 % in terms of the year-on-year rate of change in CPI, and the APP is set to be on an ongoing basis without any termination date from 2014. Prime Minister Shinzo Abe describes these policy innovations as a "regime change." The market, however, does not respond to this "regime change" strongly. JGB yields remain roughly unchanged across the board, and OIS rates only decline moderately at 20-year maturity. Prime Minister Shinzo Abe's first attempt, therefore, fails to bring interest rates further down.

Empirical evidence accumulated over the large set of CME-related events show that the CME program is effective in lowering interest rates at intermediate term

---

[16] Prime Minister Shinzo Abe campaigns on the platform of "Abenomics," and thus it is widely speculated that the new government would risk the BOJ's independences (Fawley and Neely 2013). The ruling Liberal Democratic Party even threatens to rewrite the law to make the BOJ more obedient if the central bank fails to follow quickly with bold measures to achieve the 2 % inflation target.

Table 4.7 Two-day changes in Japanese government bond yields, OIS rates, and yield-OIS spreads

Event date	Change	1-year	2-year	3-year	5-year	7-year	10-year	20-year	30-year
1. December 2, 2008 (SFSO)	Δ(JGB yield)	-3	-3	-3	0	-1	-5	-4	-2
	Δ(OIS rate)	0	0	N.A.	N.A.	N.A.	N.A.	N.A.	N.A.
	Δ(Yield-OIS spread)	-3	-4	N.A.	N.A.	N.A.	N.A.	N.A.	N.A.
2. December 19, 2008 (OAP)	Δ(JGB yield)	-7	-6	-6	-4	-4	-4	-8	-13
	Δ(OIS rate)	-2	-3	0	N.A.	N.A.	N.A.	N.A.	N.A.
	Δ(Yield-OIS spread)	-5	-3	-6	N.A.	N.A.	N.A.	N.A.	N.A.
3. January 22, 2009 (OAP)	Δ(JGB yield)	0	0	-3	-3	-3	1	5	4
	Δ(OIS rate)	-1	1	N.A.	N.A.	N.A.	N.A.	N.A.	N.A.
	Δ(Yield-OIS spread)	0	-1	N.A.	N.A.	N.A.	N.A.	N.A.	N.A.
4. February 3, 2009 (OAP)	Δ(JGB yield)	1	3	5	5	8	5	4	3
	Δ(OIS rate)	-1	0	N.A.	N.A.	N.A.	N.A.	N.A.	N.A.
	Δ(Yield-OIS spread)	2	3	N.A.	N.A.	N.A.	N.A.	N.A.	N.A.
5. February 19, 2009 (SFSO/OAP)	Δ(JGB yield)	0	1	-1	0	1	2	3	3
	Δ(OIS rate)	1	0	N.A.	N.A.	N.A.	N.A.	N.A.	N.A.
	Δ(Yield-OIS spread)	-1	1	N.A.	N.A.	N.A.	N.A.	N.A.	N.A.
6. March 18, 2009 (OAP)	Δ(JGB yield)	-1	-1	-4	-6	-9	-4	-1	1
	Δ(OIS rate)	1	-1	N.A.	N.A.	N.A.	N.A.	N.A.	N.A.
	Δ(Yield-OIS spread)	-2	0	N.A.	N.A.	N.A.	N.A.	N.A.	N.A.
7. July 15, 2009 (SFSO/OAP)	Δ(JGB yield)	0	2	1	0	-1	0	2	2
	Δ(OIS rate)	0	1	0	N.A.	N.A.	N.A.	N.A.	N.A.
	Δ(Yield-OIS spread)	0	1	1	N.A.	N.A.	N.A.	N.A.	N.A.
8. October 30, 2009 (SFSO/FRO)	Δ(JGB yield)	0	-1	-1	-2	-3	-3	-4	-5
	Δ(OIS rate)	1	0	-1	-3	-4	-4	-6	-6
	Δ(Yield-OIS spread)	-1	-1	-1	1	1	1	2	0
9. December 1, 2009 (FRO)	Δ(JGB yield)	-4	-5	-6	-6	-5	-5	-5	-5
	Δ(OIS rate)	-4	-4	-6	-5	-3	-2	0	1
	Δ(Yield-OIS spread)	0	-1	0	-2	-2	-3	-6	-6

(continued)

Table 4.7 (continued)

Event date	Change	1-year	2-year	3-year	5-year	7-year	10-year	20-year	30-year
10. December 18, 2009 (PST)	Δ(JGB yield)	−1	−1	−2	−6	−5	−3	−5	−4
	Δ(OIS rate)	−1	−1	−1	−2	−2	−3	−3	−4
	Δ(Yield-OIS spread)	0	0	−1	−4	−3	0	−1	0
11. March 17, 2010 (FRO)	Δ(JGB yield)	0	0	2	3	5	2	0	0
	Δ(OIS rate)	0	0	1	2	2	3	4	5
	Δ(Yield-OIS spread)	0	0	1	1	2	−1	−3	−5
12. April 30, 2010 (GSFF)	Δ(JGB yield)	1	0	1	0	−1	−1	−2	−3
	Δ(OIS rate)	0	0	0	−1	1	1	1	1
	Δ(Yield-OIS spread)	0	0	1	1	−1	−1	−3	−4
13. May 21, 2010 (GSFF)	Δ(JGB yield)	0	0	1	1	0	0	−2	−3
	Δ(OIS rate)	0	−1	1	0	−1	−2	−4	−5
	Δ(Yield-OIS spread)	0	1	0	−1	1	1	2	2
14. June 15, 2010 (GSFF)	Δ(JGB yield)	0	0	0	−1	1	1	1	2
	Δ(OIS rate)	0	0	0	−5	0	−1	−1	−1
	Δ(Yield-OIS spread)	0	0	0	4	2	2	2	3
15. August 30, 2010 (FRO)	Δ(JGB yield)	0	−1	−1	−3	−5	−4	−3	−3
	Δ(OIS rate)	−1	−1	−2	−2	−3	−3	−2	−2
	Δ(Yield-OIS spread)	−1	0	1	−1	−1	−1	−1	−1
16. October 5, 2010 (CME)	Δ(JGB yield)	−1	−1	−2	−5	−7	−10**	−3	−1
	Δ(OIS rate)	−1	−1	0	−6	−6	−8	−6	−5
	Δ(Yield-OIS spread)	0	0	−2	1	0	−1	3	4
17. October 28, 2010 (CME)	Δ(JGB yield)	1	0	0	0	0	−2	1	0
	Δ(OIS rate)	1	0	0	−2	−2	−3	−3	−4
	Δ(Yield-OIS spread)	−1	0	0	1	2	1	4	4
18. November 5, 2010 (CME)	Δ(JGB yield)	1	−1	−2	3	5	4	5	5
	Δ(OIS rate)	1	1	3	4	2	3	4	3
	Δ(Yield-OIS spread)	0	1	3	−1	2	1	1	1

19. March 14, 2011 (CME)	Δ(JGB yield)	1	0	0	0	-4	-9	-3	5	6
	Δ(OIS rate)	-2	-5	-5	-5	-9	-8	-6	-5	-4
	Δ(Yield-OIS spread)	3	5	5	5	5	-1	3	10	10
20. April 28, 2011 (DA)	Δ(JGB yield)	0	-1	-1	-1	-2	-1	-1	0	0
	Δ(OIS rate)	-2	-1	0	0	-3	-1	-1	-3	-2
	Δ(Yield-OIS spread)	2	0	1	3	1	-1	0	3	2
21. June 14, 2011 (GSFF)	Δ(JGB yield)	0	0	0	0	3	4	2	-1	-1
	Δ(OIS rate)	0	0	0	0	0	0	1	0	0
	Δ(Yield-OIS spread)	0	1	2	2	3	4	1	-1	-1
22. August 4, 2011 (CME)	Δ(JGB yield)	0	-1	-1	-1	-1	-1	-1	0	-1
	Δ(OIS rate)	1	0	0	0	1	1	1	0	-1
	Δ(Yield-OIS spread)	-2	-1	-1	-2	-2	-2	-2	0	0
23. October 27, 2011 (CME)	Δ(JGB yield)	0	0	1	3	3	5	5	3	3
	Δ(OIS rate)	1	1	1	3	3	5	6	7	9
	Δ(Yield-OIS spread)	-1	-1	0	-1	-1	0	-1	-3	-6
24. February 14, 2012 (CME)	Δ(JGB yield)	-1	-1	-2	-2	-2	-2	-1	0	0
	Δ(OIS rate)	0	0	4	4	-2	-3	-3	1	2
	Δ(Yield-OIS spread)	-1	-2	-5	-5	0	1	1	-1	-2
25. March 13, 2012 (GSFF)	Δ(JGB yield)	0	0	0	0	2	5	3	1	0
	Δ(OIS rate)	0	0	1	1	4	5	6	5	5
	Δ(Yield-OIS spread)	0	-1	-1	-1	-2	-1	-2	-4	-5
26. April 27, 2012 (CME)	Δ(JGB yield)	0	0	-2	-2	-2	-3	-3	-3	-3
	Δ(OIS rate)	0	0	0	0	-1	-1	-2	-4	-4
	Δ(Yield-OIS spread)	0	0	-2	-2	-1	-2	-1	1	1
27. July 12, 2012 (CME)	Δ(JGB yield)	0	0	0	0	0	1	-1	-1	-2
	Δ(OIS rate)	0	0	1	1	-1	-1	-1	-2	-2
	Δ(Yield-OIS spread)	0	0	-1	-1	0	1	-1	0	0

(continued)

Table 4.7 (continued)

Event date	Change	1-year	2-year	3-year	5-year	7-year	10-year	20-year	30-year
28. September 19, 2012 (CME)	Δ(JGB yield)	0	0	−1	−1	−1	−1	−1	0
	Δ(OIS rate)	0	0	0	1	−3	−1	−1	0
	Δ(Yield-OIS spread)	0	0	0	−2	2	0	0	1
29. October 30, 2012 (CME/SBLF)	Δ(JGB yield)	0	0	0	1	0	0	0	0
	Δ(OIS rate)	0	0	0	0	1	1	1	2
	Δ(Yield-OIS spread)	0	0	0	1	−1	−1	−1	−1
30. December 20, 2012 (CME/SBLF)	Δ(JGB yield)	0	0	0	−1	−2	−2	−3	−5
	Δ(OIS rate)	0	0	0	0	−1	−1	−3	−4
	Δ(Yield-OIS spread)	0	0	0	−1	−1	−1	0	−1
31. January 22, 2013 (CME)	Δ(JGB yield)	1	1	1	1	1	0	−1	0
	Δ(OIS rate)	1	2	1	0	1	2	−6	0
	Δ(Yield-OIS spread)	0	−1	0	1	0	−2	5	−1
32. April 4, 2013 (QQME)	Δ(JGB yield)	2	3	3	4	11	−2	−24	−28
	Δ(OIS rate)	0	0	2	5	3	−5	−15	−17
	Δ(Yield-OIS spread)	2	3	1	0	7	3	−9	−11
SFSO-related events	Δ(JGB yield)	−3	−2	−4	−3	−3	−5	−3	−2
	Δ(OIS rate)	2	1	N.A.	N.A.	N.A.	N.A.	N.A.	N.A.
	Δ(Yield-OIS spread)	−5	−3	N.A.	N.A.	N.A.	N.A.	N.A.	N.A.
OAP-related events	Δ(JGB yield)	−8	−2	−8	−9	−7	1	4	0
	Δ(OIS rate)	−2	−2	N.A.	N.A.	N.A.	N.A.	N.A.	N.A.
	Δ(Yield-OIS spread)	−6	0	N.A.	N.A.	N.A.	N.A.	N.A.	N.A.
FRO-related events	Δ(JGB yield)	−5	−7	−7	−9	−8	−9	−12	−14
	Δ(OIS rate)	−4	−4	−7	−8	−8	−6	−4	−1
	Δ(Yield-OIS spread)	−1	−2	1	−1	0	−3	−8	−12
GSFF-related events	Δ(JGB yield)	−1	0	5	5	9	5	−3	−6
	Δ(OIS rate)	0	0	2	−2	5	4	1	0
	Δ(Yield-OIS spread)	0	1	3	7	5	1	−4	−6

CME-related events								
Δ(JGB yield)	0	-3	-4	-10	-15	-16	2	3
Δ(OIS rate)	1	-4	-1	-16	-16	-13	-16	-7
Δ(Yield-OIS spread)	0	2	-3	6	1	-2	19	10
Total net change in JGB yield	-13	-14	-16	-26	-18	-29	-41	-50
Total net change in JGB yield (since October 2009)	-3	-9	-5	-18	-10	-25	-41	-48
Total net change in JPY OIS rate (since October 2009)	-5	-11	-5	-26	-19	-24	-41	-31
Total net change in yield-OIS spread (since October 2009)	2	3	0	8	9	-1	-1	-17

Notes: All changes are measured in basis points. Cumulative changes may differ from the sum of changes reported for individual events because of rounding. SFSO represents special fund-supplying operation; OAP represents outright asset purchase; FRO represents fixed-rate operation; PST represents price stability target; GSFF represents growth-supporting funding facility; CME represents comprehensive monetary easing; and SBLF represents simulating bank lending facility. ***, **, and * indicate changes in interest rate outside the 0.5th and 99.5th percentile range, the 1st and 99th percentile range, and the 2.5th and 97.5th percentile range of the distribution of interest rate changes in normal time, respectively with maturities between 5 and 10 years. Marginal decline in interest rates is also found for JGBs with shorter maturities. In contrast, longer-term JGB yields increase cumulatively over the set of CME-related events. This is largely attributable to the fact that the assets acquired under the APP focus mainly on those with shorter maturities. Moreover, looking at the series of CME-related events suggests that adjusting policy measures bit by bit is unlikely to affect market interest rates effectively. Even the fairly radical changes in monetary policy under "Abenomics" fail to bring interest rates further down. Therefore, innovative ways of thinking about the design and conduct of monetary policy are clearly needed. Besides, the decomposition of changes in interest rates suggests that the decline in shorter- and medium-term JGB yields over the set of CME-related events is more likely to be attributable to the decrease in OIS rates through the signaling channel.

4.5.3.7   BOJ's QQME-Related Event (Event 32)

To better implement his "Abenomics," Prime Minister Shinzo Abe nominates Mr. Haruhiko Kuroda, who is also an advocate of more aggressive monetary policy, to lead the Japanese central bank. After the first Policy Board meeting chaired by the newly appointed governor on April 4, 2013, the BOJ unveils a massive QQME program, which is believed to be the boldest monetary experiment in modern times. Under the new program, the central bank shifts its main operating target for money market operations from its policy rate to the monetary base, with an intention to double the monetary base in 2 years to achieve the 2 % price stability target at earliest possible time. Specifically, the central bank will increase its monetary base at an annual pace of about ¥60 trillion to ¥70 trillion, and increase the outstanding amount of its JGBs holdings at an annual pace of about ¥50 trillion which is equivalent of almost 10 % of Japan's GDP. The average remaining maturity of JGB purchases will also be doubled. In addition, the central bank aims to double the outstanding amounts of ETFs purchased in 2 years as well. The BOJ, therefore, enters a new phase of monetary easing both in terms of quantity and quality. Although Mr. Haruhiko Kuroda has previously indicated that he would do "whatever it takes" to achieve the inflation target and stimulate the economy, the bold measures under the QQME program are more than what have been widely expected in the market. The dramatic moves clearly show that Mr. Haruhiko Kuroda's approach is rather different from the previous approaches adopted by the BOJ which are characterized by a series of regular policy changes. Instead, he adopts a "big bang" approach which takes all available steps to maximize the market impact. However, the market is concerned about the risk of asset bubbles which might be created by such an aggressive monetary policy.

Market interest rates on the long end of the yield curve respond positively to such an unprecedented burst of monetary stimulus. JGB yields at 30- and 20-year maturities experience their largest 2-day falls over the large set of QE-related events, declining significantly by 28 and 24 basis points, respectively. In contrast, JGB yields at medium and shorter maturities rise slightly. A similar pattern is also observed for OIS rates, which indicates that the signaling channel plays a relatively more important role than the portfolio rebalance channel in transmitting the impact of the QQME program into market interest rates. Besides, the 1-day changes reported in Appendix D show that there might be some overreactions to the introduction of the QQME program on the event day which are subsequently reversed on the day after. Taking the benchmark 10-year JGB yield for example, it falls sharply by 11 basis points hitting its record low immediately after the announcement, but rebounds significantly by 9 basis points on the following day. This may indicate that it takes longer time for the market to thoroughly evaluate and fully absorb the effect of such dramatic moves in the central bank's monetary policy.

4.5.3.8   Other BOJ's QE-Related Events (Events 10 and 20)

Apart from the accommodative monetary policy measures summarized above, the BOJ also carries out some other unconventional operations. On December 18, 2009, the central bank clarifies its medium- to long-term price stability target by eliminating the acceptability of zero inflation. More precisely, the BOJ's price stability target is expressed as "in a positive range of 2 percent or lower with a midpoint of around 1 percent" (see, for example, Shirai 2013). The clarification of the central bank's inflation target is followed by decline in JGB yields across all maturities. The fall in medium- and longer-term interest rates is relatively more evident. The same pattern is observed in the change in OIS rates, which clearly shows that the clarification of the inflation target affects interest rates through the signaling channel. In response to the new government's desire, the BOJ raises the price stability target to 2 % on January 22, 2013. However, the rise in price stability target does not induce further fall in interest rates.

In response to the great east Japan earthquake that occurred in March 2011, the BOJ introduces a funds-supplying operation that aims to provide financial institutions in disaster area with longer-term funds for restoration and rebuilding. The operation with a total amount of ¥1 trillion in loans is established on April 28, 2011. However, market response to the release of the news is rather weak.

In addition, on October 30, 2012, the BOJ announces its intention to provide long-term funds, up to the amount equivalent to the net increase in lending, at a low interest rate to financial institutions at their request. The operational details of the stimulating bank lending facility (SBLF) are released on December 20, 2012. Through this facility, unlimited loans at maturities between 1 and 3 years are available and are allowed to be rolled over to have a maximum duration of 4 years. Both of the SBLF-related announcements are overlapped with the expansion of the CME, and thus their effect on interest rates cannot be isolated.

4.5.3.9   Cumulative Changes Over BOJ's QE-Related Events (Events 1–31)

Despite the enormous efforts made by the BOJ, our empirical results reported in Table 4.7 show that the central bank's unconventional monetary policy measures are

relatively less effective in lowering interest rates. On average, JGB yields decline by
about 45 basis points at longer maturities, about 25 basis points at medium maturities, and about 15 basis points at shorter maturities. The cumulative decline in JGB
yields over the large set of BOJ's QE-related events is less than one-third the size of
that observed on government bond yields in the USA and the UK over the same
period of time. However, it is reasonable to argue that interest rate levels in Japan are
much lower than those in the other major advanced economies before the start of QE
in 2008, and thus JGB yields have limited room to further decline over the QE period.

Although the OIS rates based on JPY are not available at most of the maturities
in 2008 and 2009, the empirical evidence accumulated after October 2009 clearly
shows that the limited impact of the BOJ's QE on JGB yields works primarily
through the signaling channel. No significant decline in spreads between JGB yields
and their corresponding OIS rates is found, except the one at 30-year maturity,
implying that the QE-related events have little impact on lowering the term premium component of JGB yields at almost all maturities. Our new results related to
the QE transmission mechanism in Japan are in line with those documented in the
existing literature on the first round of Japanese QE in the early 2000s (see, for
example, Ugai 2006). The relative importance of the signaling channel in transmitting the BOJ's monetary easing is likely to be attributable to the forward guidance
policy which has been implemented by the central bank as early as in 2001.

The event study offered in this section also represents one of the first attempts to
preliminarily evaluate the effect of "Abenomics." Our empirical results show that,
even though the central bank changes the settings of the CME program dramatically
in accordance with "Abenomics," the extension of the monetary easing measures
within the existing framework fails to deliver desired results. The incremental
approach is proven, once again, to be ineffective. The newly appointed governor
Haruhiko Kuroda, therefore, abandons the incremental approach and adopts a "big
bang" approach by utilizing every possible resource bestowed upon the central bank
to achieve its policy targets. Our results suggest that the "big bang" approach indeed
conveys a strong signal to the market that the BOJ will do whatever is necessary to
overcome deflation. As a result, both JGB yields and OIS rates fall significantly at
longer maturities around the introduction of the QQME. Nevertheless, since it typically takes considerable time before the effects of the aggressive monetary policy
permeate the whole economy, the overall impact of "Abenomics" should be better
examined in a longer period of time.

In addition, the 1-day changes in JGB yields, OIS rates, and yield-OIS spreads
around the set of BOJ's QE-related events are reported in Appendix D. Unlike the
evidence from the USA and the UK, the 1-day changes in JGB yields are similar to
their 2-day counterparts in terms of sign and size. This is likely due to the fact that
the BOJ has a long history of adopting the QE policy. The market participants in
Japan are more familiar with the unconventional monetary policies, and thus are
able to revise their expectations more quickly according to the news released.
However, some evidence of market overreactions is found in the recent introduction
of the QQME program, which is believed to be the boldest monetary experiment in
modern times.

4.5.4   Evidence from the Euro Area

4.5.4.1   Euro Area Government Bond Yields (January 1, 2008–December 31, 2012)

Figure 4.4 depicts the movements in the yields of euro area government bonds (EAGBs) at different maturities over the period from January 2008 to December 2012. The vertical lines represent the set of the ECB's QE-related events listed in Table 4.4. It clearly shows that, comparing their levels at the end of 2012 to those before the start of QE at beginning of 2008, the spreads between EAGBs at longer and shorter maturities widen significantly. The spread between 30- and 1-year EAGB yields increases from around 100 basis points to around 300 basis points. A substantial reduction in spreads is observed in the late 2011, which is likely to be caused by the escalating European sovereign debt crisis. Overall, there is a noticeable decline in EAGB yields at shorter maturities over the period. The decline in EAGB yields at longer maturities, however, is less obvious. To assess the impact of the ECB's unconventional monetary policies on interest rates, we focus on the 2-day change in EAGB yields right around each of the QE-related events. Empirical evidence from the euro area is reported in Table 4.8.

4.5.4.2   ECB's LTRO-Related Events (Events 1–3 and 9)

The ECB is the first, among the major central banks, to adopt unconventional monetary policies in an attempt to accommodate heightened demand for liquidity caused by the recent global economic crisis. On March 28, 2008, the ECB's Governing Council decides to introduce its new supplementary LTROs with a maturity of 6 months, and further conduct supplementary LTROs with a 3-month maturity. The LTROs are carried out through a variable rate standard tender procedure with predetermined amounts (€25 billion for each of the two 6-month LTROs and €50 billion for each of the two 3-month LTROs).[17] Although EAGB yields at longer maturities fall slightly around this event, the impact of the announcement on interest rates is not obvious.

After the failure of Lehman Brothers in September 2008, the tension in money market reaches an unprecedented level. On October 15, 2008, the ECB announces that it would provide unlimited liquidity to ease the market condition. To this end, the central bank decides to conduct all of the refinancing operations with a fixed-rate tender procedure and full allotment, and expand its list of eligible collateral.[18]

---

[17] The ECB defines the variable rate tender procedure as a standard tender procedure whereby the counterparties bid both the amount of money they want to transact with the central bank and the interest rate at which they want to enter into the transaction.

[18] The fixed-rate tender procedure is defined as a tender procedure in which the interest rate is specified in advance by the central bank and in which participating counterparties bid the amount of money they want to transact at that interest rate.

Table 4.8 Two-day changes in euro area government bond yields, OIS rates, and yield-OIS spreads

Event date	Change	1-year	2-year	3-year	5-year	7-year	10-year	20-year	30-year
1. March 28, 2008 (LTRO)	Δ(EAGB yield)	1	2	2	1	1	−1	−4	−5
	Δ(OIS rate)	2	2	4	0	−3	−4	N.A.	N.A.
	Δ(Yield-OIS spread)	−1	−1	−2	2	3	3	N.A.	N.A.
2. October 15, 2008 (LTRO)	Δ(EAGB yield)	−8	−13	−14	−9	−3	4	17	23
	Δ(OIS rate)	−16	−26	−16	−16	−11	−5	2	5
	Δ(Yield-OIS spread)	8	12	2	7	7	9	15	17
3. May 7, 2009 (CBPP/LTRO)	Δ(EAGB yield)	−6	−5	−3	2	5	9**	16	18
	Δ(OIS rate)	−8	−4	2	15	20	25	25	21
	Δ(Yield-OIS spread)	2	−2	−5	−13	−15	−16	−9	−3
4. June 4, 2009 (CBPP)	Δ(EAGB yield)	17	26	26	22	17	10**	1	13
	Δ(OIS rate)	19	30	36	25	21	17	11	7
	Δ(Yield-OIS spread)	−2	−5	−10	−3	−4	−7	−10	7
5. May 10, 2010 (SMP)	Δ(EAGB yield)	−12	−15	−16	−15	−12	−7	5	9
	Δ(OIS rate)	−2	2	6	5	12	16	28	33
	Δ(Yield-OIS spread)	−10	−16	−22	−20	−24	−23	−24	−24
6. June 30, 2010 (CBPP)	Δ(EAGB yield)	5	5	4	2	−1	−4	−5	−5
	Δ(OIS rate)	9	10	8	1	−1	−2	−1	−1
	Δ(Yield-OIS spread)	−4	−5	−4	0	−1	−2	−4	−4
7. October 6, 2011 (CBPP)	Δ(EAGB yield)	1	2	1	0	1	2	4	5
	Δ(OIS rate)	8	9	8	7	7	7	5	3
	Δ(Yield-OIS spread)	−8	−7	−7	−7	−6	−5	−1	2
8. November 3, 2011 (CBPP)	Δ(EAGB yield)	4	1	2	4	6	9**	13	15
	Δ(OIS rate)	−4	−3	−5	−2	0	2	5	0
	Δ(Yield-OIS spread)	9	5	8	6	6	7	8	15
9. December 8, 2011 (LTRO)	Δ(EAGB yield)	13	11	10	10	10	12**	13	14
	Δ(OIS rate)	−1	2	−2	6	3	2	−1	4
	Δ(Yield-OIS spread)	13	9	12	3	7	9	14	10

10. August 2, 2012 (OMT)								
Δ(EAGB yield)	−21	−21	−17	−9	−2	5	16	20
Δ(OIS rate)	4	4	3	6	7	5	5	4
Δ(Yield-OIS spread)	−25	−25	−20	−15	−10	1	12	16
11. September 6, 2012 (OMT)								
Δ(EAGB yield)	−2	−7	−13	−18	−18	−16***	−12	−11
Δ(OIS rate)	1	3	3	6	8	8	11	11
Δ(Yield-OIS spread)	−3	−10	−16	−25	−26	−23	−23	−22
LTRO-related events								
Δ(EAGB yield)	−1	−6	−5	4	13	24	43	50
Δ(OIS rate)	−23	−25	−12	5	11	19	N.A.	N.A.
Δ(Yield-OIS spread)	22	19	7	−1	3	6	N.A.	N.A.
CBPP-related events								
Δ(EAGB yield)	21	29	31	29	28	26	30	47
Δ(OIS rate)	24	43	49	46	47	48	46	30
Δ(Yield-OIS spread)	−4	−14	−18	−16	−19	−22	−16	17
OMT-related events								
Δ(EAGB yield)	−23	−28	−30	−27	−20	−10	4	9
Δ(OIS rate)	5	7	6	12	15	13	15	15
Δ(Yield-OIS spread)	−28	−35	−36	−39	−35	−23	−11	−6
Total net change in EAGB yield	−9	−14	−17	−11	3	24	66	97
Total net change in EAGB yield (since October 2008)	−10	−16	−18	−12	3	25	70	102
Total net change in EUR OIS rate (since October 2008)	11	28	44	53	67	75	91	87
Total net change in yield-OIS spread (since October 2008)	−21	−43	−63	−65	−64	−50	−21	14

Notes: All changes are measured in basis points. Cumulative changes may differ from the sum of changes reported for individual events because of rounding. LTRO represents longer-term refinancing operation; CBPP represents covered bonds purchase programs; SMP represents securities markets program; and OMT represents outright monetary transaction. ***, **, and * indicate changes in interest rate outside the 0.5th and 99.5th percentile range, the 1st and 99th percentile range, and the 2.5th and 97.5th percentile range of the distribution of interest rate changes in normal time, respectively

This new procedure allows the market to determine the amount of liquidity to be provided by the central bank at the primary policy rate rather than the central bank predetermines the amount of funds available and auction the funds by price. As a result, EAGB yields and OIS rates at shorter maturities fall considerably by more than 10 and 18 basis points, respectively, reflecting a revised expectation about future short rates. EAGB yields at longer maturities, however, increase substantially around the event by about 20 basis points. The mixed impact of the new tender procedure on interest rates is largely due to the fact that only short-term liquidity is expected to be provided to the market through the LTROs.

The LTROs are subsequently expanded twice in 2009 and 2011. On May 7, 2009, the ECB decides to undertake three LTROs with a maturity of 12 months to accommodate the financial institutions' demand for longer-term liquidity. On December 8, 2011, two LTROs with a maturity of 36 months are introduced with an option of early repayment after 1 year. The expansions of LTROs provide unlimited liquidity with relatively longer terms to the market but fail to reduce interest rates, as no significant declines in EAGB yields are evidenced around these two events. In fact, interest rates on the long end of the curve further increase substantially. The rise in longer-term EAGB yields is likely to be caused by the dramatic increase in yields of government bonds of those countries with high credit and liquidity risks such as Greece, Ireland, and Portugal.

In summary, our results show that the LTRO-related events do not bring down EAGB yields at most of the maturities. EAGB yields fall marginally at shorter maturities, but rise substantially at longer maturities. Significant decline in OIS rate is only found on the short end of the yield curve, suggesting that the LTROs lower market expectation about interest rates in the near future. The mixed empirical evidence is likely because the LTROs provide unlimited liquidity but only with maturities less than 3 years. However, the fall in expectations about future policy rate at shorter maturities is largely offset by the rise in term premium which may reflect the increased credit and liquidity risks amid the European sovereign debt crisis.

4.5.4.3   ECB's CBPP-Related Events (Events 3, 4, and 6–8)

The failure of Lehman Brothers in September 2008 also seriously impairs the covered bond market. The ECB's Governing Council judges that the covered bond market is one of the most affected segments of the private securities markets. Accordingly, on May 7, 2009, the ECB decides to purchase around €60 billion in covered bonds to revive the market, and simultaneously cut the policy rate and launch 12-month LTROs.[19] Following up the initial announcement, the technical

---

[19] Fawley and Neely (2013) clarify the features of the covered bonds by highlighting that covered bonds differ from other asset-backed securities in two ways. First, in the event of bond default, covered bond-holders have recourse to the issuer of the bond, as well as the underlying collateral pool (thus the term "covered"). Second, banks must hold the underlying collateral on their balance sheet, which reduces the incentives to make and securitize low-quality loans.

modalities of the CBPP are released on June 4, 2009. Although it to some extent compresses the spread between EAGB yields and OIS rates, the launch of the CBPP fails to encourage decline in interest rate levels. Both EAGB yields and OIS rates increase substantially for almost all maturities around the events, reflecting rising expectations about future interest rates. On June 30, 2010, the purchases of €60 billion in covered bonds from both primary and secondary markets are fully completed, and the Eurosystem central banks indicate that they intend to hold the purchased covered bonds until maturity. This announcement is followed by slight decline in interest rates on the long end but marginal increase in those at the short end. The transmission mechanism through which the market is affected by the event, however, is not clearly shown in our results.

In response to the escalating European sovereign debt crisis, the ECB decides, on October 6, 2011, to launch the second round of the CBPP (CBPP2) under which about €40 billion in covered bonds would be purchased. The operational details of the CBPP2 are released on November 3, 2011, which specifies that the covered bonds to be purchased are set to have a maximum residual of 10.5 years. Since the CBPP2 is implemented with the intention to revive the particular segment of the private securities markets, it does not reduce EAGB yields.

All in together, EAGB yields rise cumulatively by about 30 basis points over the whole set of CBPP-related events, while OIS rates increase cumulatively by over 40 basis points. The spreads between EAGB yields and their corresponding OIS rate thus fall at almost all maturities. These empirical results indicate that, although the CBPP-related events see substantial increase in market interest rates, they reduce the term premium in EAGB yields significantly. The rise in market interest rates reflects the upward revision of the expected future short rates in response to the global financial crisis as well as the European sovereign debt crisis.

4.5.4.4   ECB's SMP-Related Event (Event 5)

In the second quarter of 2010, the severe tensions caused by the European sovereign debt crisis hamper the transmission mechanism of the central bank's monetary policy. The ECB decides, on May 10, 2010, to conduct interventions in both public and private debt securities markets in the euro area through an SMP. The scope of the program is not preannounced, but the Governing Council indicates that it would be determined by taking into account the financial position of the euro area governments. It is worth noting that asset purchases under the SMP are set to be sterilized by conducting specific operations to reabsorb the liquidity injected into the markets, and thus would not increase monetary base. Accordingly, Fawley and Neely (2013) argue that the SMP does not fall under the usual definition of QE.

Since the SMP allows the ECB to purchase euro area government debts from the secondary market, EAGB yields fall significantly at shorter and medium maturities around the announcement, by about 13 basis points. In addition, the spreads between EAGB yields and their corresponding OIS rates also decline considerably across all maturities, which indicates that the SMP depresses interest rates primarily by lowering their term premiums through the portfolio rebalance channel. However, the OIS rates, which reflect the market expectation about the path of future short rates, increase at almost all maturities around the event.

4.5.4.5 ECB's OMT-Related Events (Events 10 and 11)

Concerned with the solvency of Spain and Italy, the ECB's President Mario Draghi indicates, in a press conference held on August 2, 2012, that the central bank intends to expand its sovereign debt purchases. He also directly addresses concerns over the viability of the euro by proclaiming that "the euro is irreversible" (Fawley and Neely 2013). As a consequence, EAGB yields also fall significantly around the press conference at shorter maturities. Similar pattern is also found for the yield-OIS spreads, indicating that expansion in sovereign debt purchases lowers interest rate through the portfolio rebalance channel.

The new plan for buying bonds from euro area countries, which is known as OMTs, is formally announced by the Governing Council on September 6, 2012, to replace the SMP. Unlike the SMP which is a temporary measure, the OMTs have no predetermined time and size limit. But the liquidity created through the OMTs will be fully sterilized as with the SMP transactions, and thus will not increase monetary base. The release of the operational details for OMTs is followed by noticeable declines in both EAGB yields and yield-OIS spreads at almost all maturities, which confirms that the portfolio rebalance channel is operative.

Taken together, the OMT-related events have significant effect on interest rates, bringing down EAGB yields at shorter and medium maturities by over 20 basis points. The spreads between EAGB yields and their corresponding OIS rates also fall considerably at all maturities. Our empirical evidence, therefore, suggests that the OMTs are effective in lowering interest rate through the portfolio rebalance channel.

4.5.4.6 Cumulative Changes Over ECB's QE-Related Events (Events 1–11)

According to our results, the ECB's unconventional monetary policies have mixed impact on market interest rates at different maturities. On average, EAGB yields with maturities less than 5 years decline moderately by about 13 basis points, while those with maturities over 10 years rise substantially by more than 60 basis points. The decomposition of interest rate responses shows that market expectation about future short rates, as proxied by the OIS rates, rises across all maturities, while term premiums, as reflected by the yield-OIS spreads, fall at almost all maturities. It appears that the ECB's QE-related events are useful in reducing the term premium of interest rates through the portfolio rebalance channel, but the fall in term premium is largely offset by the rise in market expectation about future short rates.

Overall, our empirical results show that the unconventional monetary policies adopted by the ECB are less effective in terms of reducing government bond yields.

The ineffectiveness of these policies may, to a great extent, be attributable to the escalating sovereign debt crisis over the period under investigation. In addition, Baumeister and Benati (2010) argue that, unlike the other major central banks, the ECB does not consider the compression in the yield spread as the fundamental objective of its unconventional monetary policies. The objective function of the central bank is to save the euro by reviving particular segments of the securities markets.

One-day changes in EAGB yields, OIS rates, and yield-OIS spreads reported in Appendix E are almost consistently smaller in magnitude than their respective 2-day counterparts. The relatively longer time for the market to absorb the QE-related news, on the one hand, may be because of the relative novelty of the unconventional monetary policies; on the other hand, it may be because the transmission mechanism of the central bank's monetary policy is impaired by the European sovereign debt crisis.

4.6 Conclusion

This chapter represents one of the most comprehensive and up-to-date reviews of the unconventional monetary policies adopted by the central banks in the UK, the USA, Japan, and the euro area in response to the recent global economic crisis. The overall impact of the unconventional monetary policies on market interest rates in each of the economies is empirically assessed and summarized in Table 4.9. A number of features are of particular interest.

First, the unconventional measures undertaken by the Fed and BOE, which focus primarily on bond purchases, are much more effective in lowering interest rates than those undertaken by the BOJ and ECB, which rely more heavily on lending to private financial institutions. On balance, government bond yields in the USA and the UK decline cumulatively by over 100 basis points at medium and longer maturities, and more than 50 basis points at shorter maturities. In contrast, an average fall by only about 20 basis points is found for government bond yields in Japan, while mixed results are found for those in the euro area. Lenza et al. (2010) point out that, despite the differences in design, their operational frameworks for monetary policy across the central banks should be understood in light of the different structures of financial systems in their respective jurisdictions. Given the importance of banks as sources of external funds in Japan and the euro area, it is understandable that the BOJ and ECB choose to conduct their unconventional monetary policies mainly through the banking system. Moreover, the seemingly ineffectiveness of the conduct of unconventional monetary policies in Japan and the euro area should also be understood in light of their respective backgrounds. The relatively less significant decline in interest rates in Japan cumulative over the BOJ's QE-related events might be partially due to the fact that the interest rate levels have been lower than those of the other major advanced economies even before the start of QE, leaving JGB yields have very limited room to further decline. In Europe, the central bank's objective function is to save the euro by reviving particular segments of the securities markets

Table 4.9 International comparison of the cumulative 2-day changes in government bond yields, OIS rates, and yield-OIS spreads over QE-related events

Economy	Cumulative change	1-year	2-year	3-year	5-year	7-year	10-year	20-year	25/30-year
US	ΣΔ(US Treasury yield)	-36	-65	-74	-129	-161	-171	-124	-106
	ΣΔ(OIS rate)	-31	-58	-86	-132	-161	-163	-118	-112
	Δ(Yield-OIS spread)	-5	-7	12	3	0	-8	-6	6
UK	ΣΔ(UK gilt yield)	-30	-53	-68	-90	-96	-92	-107	-116
	ΣΔ(OIS rate)	-13	-29	-29	-20	-18	-16	-12	-10
	ΣΔ(Yield-OIS spread)	-17	-24	-39	-70	-78	-76	-95	-106
Japan	ΣΔ(JGB yield)	-13	-14	-16	-26	-18	-29	-41	-50
	ΣΔ(JGB yield) since October 2009	-3	-9	-5	-18	-10	-25	-41	-48
	ΣΔ(OIS rate) since October 2009	-5	-11	-5	-26	-19	-24	-41	-31
	ΣΔ(Yield-OIS spread) since October 2009	2	3	0	8	9	-1	-1	-17
Euro area	ΣΔ(EAGB yield)	-9	-14	-17	-11	3	24	66	97
	ΣΔ(EAGB yield) since October 2008	-10	-16	-18	-12	3	25	70	102
	ΣΔ(OIS rate) since October 2008	11	28	44	53	67	75	91	87
	ΣΔ(Yield-OIS spread) since October 2008	-21	-43	-63	-65	-64	-50	-21	14

Notes: All changes are measured in basis points. Cumulative changes may differ from the sum of changes reported for individual events because of rounding

rather than stimulate growth by lowering interest rates, and this may explain the perverse reaction of the market.

Second, although the unconventional monetary policies adopted by the Fed and BOE are similarly designed and both are proven to be effective, our empirical results show that they impact interest rates through distinct transmission mechanisms. Specifically, the decomposition of market responses to the QE-related events suggests that the decline in the US Treasury yields largely reflects changes in policy expectations, while the decline in UK gilt yields is mainly attributable to the reductions in term premiums. Therefore, the signaling channel is dominant in the QE program conducted by the Fed, and the portfolio rebalance channel plays a more important role in the conduct of the BOE's QE program. Our results are in line with those offered by Christensen and Rudebusch (2012) who posit that the contrasting channels of influence of the US and UK unconventional monetary policy might be traced to differences in policy communication and financial market structure. First, the Fed is much more willing to provide forward-looking policy guidance on interest rates which is typically absent from the BOE's announcements, and thus the signaling effect is much stronger in the USA than in the UK.[20] Second, the government bond market in the UK is relatively less liquid than that in the USA in which Treasuries are held by a broader class of international investors, and therefore the market segmentation and resulting portfolio rebalance effect are more likely in the UK than in the USA. In addition, our study reveals new evidence that the signaling channel also plays an important role in the conduct of the BOJ's unconventional policies. This finding lends additional empirical support to the argument that the relative importance of the signaling channel may depend on the central bank's communication policies, as the forward guidance has long been adopted by the BOJ since it pioneered QE in 2001.[21]

Third, our empirical evidence from the UK and the USA shows that over 80 % of the cumulative changes in government bond yields are attributable to the first round of their QE. The market responses to the subsequent rounds of QE are much less significant. This brief thus uncovers new insight that the effectiveness of the unconventional monetary policies tends to diminish once they have been implemented. One may argue that the stronger effect of QE1-related events on interest rates is partially due to the fact that relatively more announcements included in our event sets are related to the round of QE. However, if we focus only on the initial announcement of each round of QE, the diminishing effectiveness of unconventional monetary policy can still be concluded. This finding, therefore, indicates that further policy innovations might be needed for economies which have already undertaken QE, in order to more effectively stimulate their economies and keep price stability.

---

[20] Some of the Federal Reserve's announcements regarding QE explicitly contain discussion of its policy on future federal fund rates (see Krishnamurthy and Vissing-Jorgensen 2011).

[21] As early as 2001, the BOJ makes a clear commitment to maintaining its virtually zero interest rate policy until the core CPI registering stably zero percent or a year-on-year increase is met. This innovative monetary policy tool is nowadays often referred to as "forward guidance" (see Shirai 2013).

Finally, our robustness check results show that 1-day changes in interest rates are consistently much smaller than their 2-day counterparts, except for Japan. This finding suggests that market absorbs the announcements with respect to unconventional monetary policy more slowly compared with typical monetary policies. As pointed out by Krishnamurthy and Vissing-Jorgensen (2011), the sluggish market reaction to the QE-related events may, to a great extent, be because of the relative novelty of the policies and the diversity of beliefs about the mechanisms by which they operate. Given the fact that the BOJ has a long history of adopting QE policy, the market participants in Japan are more familiar with the unconventional monetary measures, and thus are able to revise their expectations more quickly according to the QE-related news released.

Chapter 5
Broader Economic Effects
of Quantitative Easing

Since the ultimate objective of quantitative easing is to stimulate economic growth and keep price stability, this chapter further assesses the wider effects of QE on a range of economic indicators, in particular output and inflation, in an attempt to address the research question of what would have happened to these major advanced economies if the unconventional monetary policies had not been undertaken by their respective central banks, i.e., the no-QE counterfactuals. Following the established methodology in the literature, we use large Bayesian vector autoregression (BVAR) models to estimate the impact of QE on the wider economy by assuming that the macroeconomic effects of QE work entirely through its impact on government bond yield spreads (see, for example, Kapetanios et al. 2012; Lenza et al. 2010; Baumeister and Benati 2010).[1] More specifically, we produce no-QE counterfactual forecasts using large BVAR models by adjusting the spreads between government bond yields and the 3-month Treasury bill rate in accordance with our empirical findings presented in the previous chapter. The no-QE counterfactuals are then compared with their corresponding baseline forecasts which incorporate the effects of QE on government bond spreads. The difference between the two scenarios is considered as the broader economic impact of the unconventional monetary policies.

5.1 BVAR Methodology

Vector autoregression (VAR) models have been widely used in macroeconomics for structural analysis and forecasting since the seminal work by Sims (1980). An important feature of VAR models is their flexibility which allows us to capture complex relationships among the macroeconomic variables. However, VAR models are

---

[1] The link between government bond spreads and macroeconomic variables is discussed in detail in Estrella (2005).

K. Hausken and M. Ncube, *Quantitative Easing and Its Impact in the US,*
Japan, the UK and Europe, SpringerBriefs in Economics,
DOI 10.1007/978-1-4614-9646-5_5, © The Author(s) 2013

often associated with the estimation of a large number of parameters, which uses up the degrees of freedom rapidly and results in wide confidence intervals for estimated coefficients. VAR applications are, therefore, typically based on a small number of variables, resulting in an omitted variable bias with adverse consequences both for structural analysis and forecasting.

To overcome the problems associated with standard VARs, we use the Bayesian method to estimate our models. The BVAR method has two main advantages. First, since our large VAR models contain about 30 variables, the Bayesian method enables us to overcome the over-parameterization problems which would otherwise be encountered if standard VARs are estimated with large dimensions. Second, the Bayesian method, which involves imposition of prior beliefs on the parameters, is useful to control for over-fitting problems while preserving the relevant information. Given those merits of BVAR, Banbura et al. (2010) conclude that it is an appropriate tool for large dynamic macroeconomic models. However, as discussed in Ciccarelli and Rebucci (2003), a main limitation of BVAR is that the choice of prior information for unknown parameters matters. In some cases, prior knowledge is either vague or nonexistent, and thus makes it difficult and subjective to specify a unique prior distribution. Therefore, we specify our prior carefully with reference to the literature.

Our large BVAR models are similar to those utilized by Kapetanios et al. (2012) and Lenza et al. (2010), which can be written as follows:

$$Y_t = \Theta_0 + \Theta_1 Y_{t-1} + \cdots + \Theta_p Y_{t-p} + e_t \qquad (5.1)$$

where Y_t represents a large vector of random variables included in our large dataset at time t, i.e., $(y_{1t}, y_{2t}, \cdots, y_{nt})'$; e_t represents an n-dimensional vector white-noise error term; Θ_0 represents an n-dimensional vector of constants; and $\Theta_1 \ldots \Theta_p$ represent $n \times n$ autoregressive parameter matrices.

As can be seen from Appendices F–I, our large dataset comprises macroeconomic and financial market variables for each of the four major advanced economies under investigation. Most of the macroeconomic and financial market variables are characterized by persistent processes, and thus a simple random walk forecast would be a good prior for such BVAR models (see, for example, Kapetanios et al. 2012; and Litterman 1986).[2] Accordingly, we choose a random walk process with drift as our prior for each of the variables in the BVAR model. The prior mean therefore can be expressed as follows:

$$Y_t = \Theta_0 + Y_{t-1} + e_t \qquad (5.2)$$

With this prior, the diagonal elements of Θ_1 shrink toward one and the remaining elements in $\Theta_1 \ldots \Theta_p$ shrink toward zero, implying that the "own" first lag is the most important predictor in every equation in the BVAR. In other words, the

---

[2] Kapetanios et al. (2012) argue that, in general, simple autoregressive or random walk models produce reasonable forecasts for macroeconomic and financial variables.

expected value of the matrix Θ_1 is $E(\Theta_1) = 1 \times I$. Additionally, we impose prior beliefs on the distribution of the coefficients by setting the moments for Θ_1 as follows:

$$E\left[\Theta_k^{(ij)}\right] = \begin{cases} 1 & if \quad i = j, k = 1 \\ 0 & otherwise \end{cases} \quad V\left[\Theta_k^{(ij)}\right] = \left(\frac{\lambda_0 \lambda_1}{\sigma_j k^{\lambda_3}}\right)^2 \quad (5.3)$$

where $\Theta_k^{(ij)}$ represents the element in position (i, j) in the matrix Θ_k; E is the expectation operator; V is variance; and λ_0, λ_1 and λ_3 are shrinkage parameters. The shrinkage parameter λ_0 determines the overall tightness of the prior on the error covariance matrix. For a loose overall prior, as λ_0 approaches 1, the conditional prior variance of the parameters converges to the sample residual covariance matrix. Smaller λ_0 implies a tighter overall prior as λ_0 approaches 0. The hyperparameter λ_1 controls the tightness of the beliefs about the random walk prior, i.e., the standard deviation of $\Theta_k^{(ij)}$ where $i = j$ and $k = 1$ ($k^{\lambda_3} = 1$ in this case). The hyperparameter λ_3 determines the speed of shrinkage for the variance of the coefficient on higher order lags as the lag length increases. The tightness around the constant in the model is jointly determined by the overall tightness λ_0 and a separate hyperparameter λ_4. Sims-Zha prior used in this chapter assumes that the weight of each variable's own lags is the same as those of other variables' lags, and thus the hyperparameter λ_2 is set to 1. Following Kapetanios et al. (2012), we set the lag order for our large BVAR models to one. Our BVARs are estimated using the entire sample for each of the four economies under investigation.

5.2 Variables and Datasets

Our large BVAR models comprise a wide range of financial and economic variables, covering consumer prices, domestic outputs, industrial production, interest rates, yield spreads, money aggregates, unemployment, house prices, oil prices, stock prices, consumer confidence, exchange rates, etc. (see Appendices F–I). The variables selected for our BVARs are similar to those utilized in Kapetanios et al. (2012).

QE programs, which inject a huge amount of money into the economy, are expected to affect monetary aggregates, interest rates, and exchange rates directly. Accordingly, we include in our models a large set of domestic variables for government bond yields, government bond yield spreads, monetary aggregates, and foreign exchange rates. Given that the objective of QE programs is to prevent deflation, stimulate real economic growth, and lower unemployment rate by boosting nominal spending and investment of companies and households, we include a set of policy target variables such as consumer price index, inflation expectation, gross domestic outputs, industrial production, and unemployment rate. To incorporate the potential effect of QE on the prices of a variety of other assets, variables for house prices and stock prices are also included in our BVAR. Higher house and stock prices may further encourage consumption and investment spending. Since QE programs may directly boost economic sentiment through the confidence channel, a proxy for consumer confidence is also included. Apart from the domestic variables, a set of foreign variables are also included in out models to capture the potential international financial and economic linkages.

Our BVAR models for the UK, the USA, and Japan are estimated using quarterly data from the first quarter of 1990 through the fourth quarter of 2012. Since most of the variables for the euro area only trace back to 2004, we use monthly data from January 2005 to December 2012 to estimate the BVAR for the euro area. We use log-levels of the variables to estimate the BVAR models except for those which are already defined as rates. The lists of variables for the USA, the UK, Japan, and euro area are provided in Appendices F–I, respectively. The transformation of the variables as well as the sources of data can also be found in these appendices.

5.3 Counterfactual Analyses

To assess the effects of the unconventional monetary policies on the key macroeconomic indicators, we compare their expected values under two scenarios, namely the QE scenario and no-QE scenario. The two counterfactual scenarios are created by adjusting the spreads between relevant government bond yields and the 3-month Treasury bill rate based on our empirical findings presented in the previous chapter. Similar approaches to examine the effects of unconventional monetary policy on macroeconomy can also be found in Kapetanios et al. (2012), Lenza et al. (2010) and Baumeister and Benati (2010). Lenza et al. (2010) argue that unconventional monetary policies affect the macroeconomy largely through their effects on interest rate spreads rather than solely or mainly through "quantity effects" in terms of money supply.[3] Therefore, the effect of the unconventional monetary policies should be quantified by examining how the reduction in these spreads is transmitted to the broader economy.

Under the QE scenario, we produce a baseline forecast for each of the macroeconomic indicators from the beginning of QE to the end of our forecast horizon using the observed path for the spreads between government bond yields and 3-month Treasury bill rate, $GBSpread_{QE,t}$. An assumption under the QE scenario is that observed spreads fully reflect the effect of the unconventional monetary policies. The conditional expectation for a generic variable y_t included in the vector Y_t under the QE scenario, therefore, can be expressed as follows:

$$E_\Theta \left(y_{t+h} \mid Y_t, GBSpread_{QE,t} \right) \tag{5.4}$$

---

[3] The analysis of unconventional monetary policies by Lenza et al. (2010), therefore, is concerned with the impact of a reduction of interest rate spreads given the level of the key policy rate, rather than changes in the key policy rate itself.

Under the no-QE scenario, we assume that government bond spreads would have been higher (or lower, depending on our empirical findings presented in the previous chapter) than the observed path over the period from the beginning of QE onwards had the unconventional monetary policies not been implemented. More precisely, we adjust government bond spreads by adding (or subtracting) the total cumulative change in government bond yields over the QE-related events to (or from) the observed government bond yield spread to create the no-QE scenario, $GBSpread_{NO\text{-}QE,t}$ (see Kapetanios et al. 2012). The conditional expectation for variable y_t under the no-QE scenario can be estimated as follows:

$$E_\Theta \left(y_{t+h} \mid Y_t, GBSpread_{No\text{-}QE,t} \right) \tag{5.5}$$

The impact of the QE for the generic variable y, D_y, therefore, can be approximated by the difference between the conditional expectations of variable y under the QE scenario and the no-QE scenario,

$$D_{y,t+h} = E_\Theta \left(y_{t+h} \mid Y_t, GBSpread_{QE,t} \right) - E_\Theta \left(y_{t+h} \mid Y_t, GBSpread_{No\text{-}QE,t} \right) \tag{5.6}$$

Following Kapetanios et al. (2012), we focus on the 10-, 5-, and 2-year government bond yield spreads to assess the potential macroeconomic impact of QE, so the adjustments for the no-QE scenario are applied to these spreads. For these simulations, we assume that, under the no-QE scenario, the increase (or decrease) in long-term government bond yields occur in the initial period of QE and remain over the forecast horizon.[4] However, the main limitation of this analysis, as noted in Kapetanios et al. (2012), is that it does not allow us to discriminate between the effects of movements in government bond spreads that come through term premium and those that come through expected future policy rates.[5]

5.4   Empirical Results

This section reports the empirical evidence on the broader economic effects of the unconventional monetary policies undertaken by the Federal Reserve, Bank of England, Bank of Japan, and European Central Bank in their respective economies. Visual comparison between the conditional forecasts for the key economic indicators under the QE scenario and no-QE scenario are provided in Figs. 5.1, 5.2, 5.3, and 5.4, in which the blue line depicts the actual path of the economic indicator, the

---

[4] Kapetanios et al. (2012) also conduct some sensitivity analysis by allowing the size of the adjustment on government bond spreads to vary over the forecast horizon, but the results under various spread adjustment profiles are broadly similar to the baseline results.

[5] Kapetanios et al. (2012) point out that the macroeconomic effects of QE may depend on the channel through which it affects bond yields, i.e., through term premium or expected future policy rates.

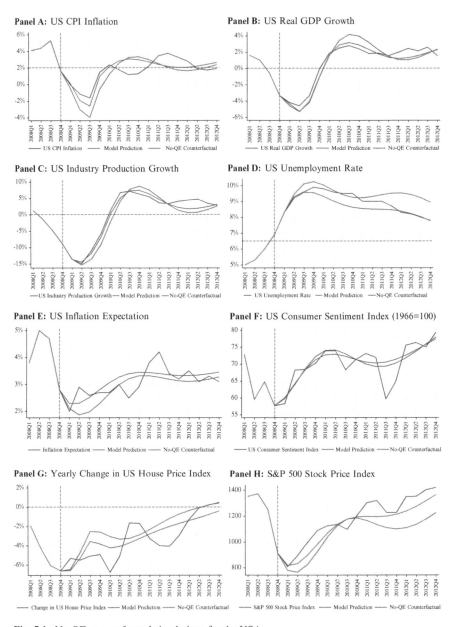

Fig. 5.1   No-QE counterfactual simulations for the USA

Panel I: Yearly Change in USD Exchange Rate Index

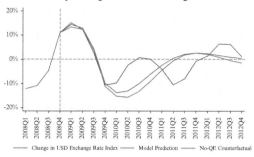

Fig. 5.1   (continued)

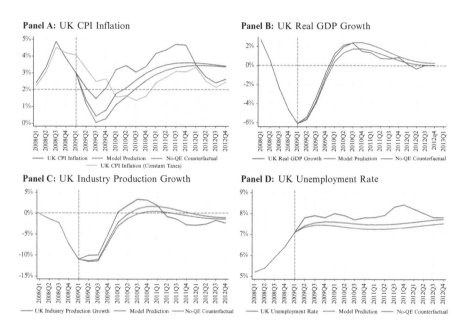

Fig. 5.2   No-QE counterfactual simulations for the UK

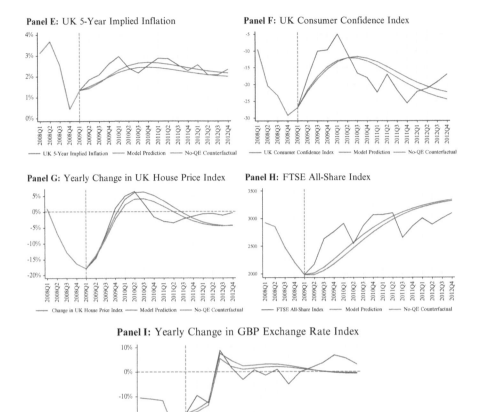

Fig. 5.2 (continued)

maroon line depicts the baseline forecast for the variable under the QE scenario, and
the green line depicts the counterfactual forecast for the variable under the no-QE
scenario. The difference between the maroon and green lines, thus, represents the
impact of QE on the underlying economic indicator. It is worth noting that, as with
any VAR model, the forecasts become less informative as the forecast horizon
lengthens.

5.4.1   *Evidence from the USA*

To conduct counterfactual analysis for the USA, we assume that under the no-QE
scenario the US Treasury yields at 2-, 5-, and 10-year maturities would have been

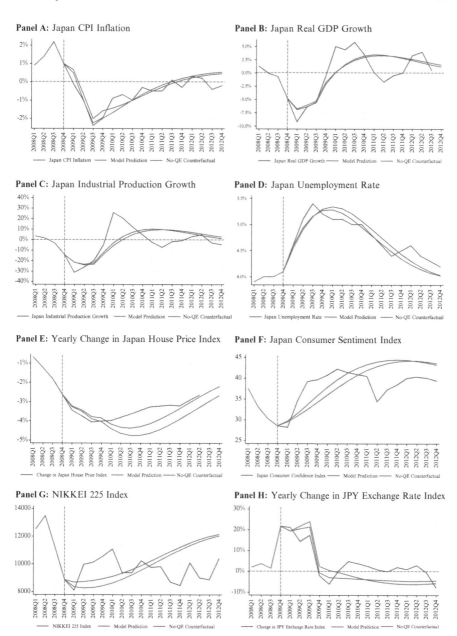

Fig. 5.3 No-QE counterfactual simulations for Japan

65 basis points, 129 basis points, and 171 basis points higher than their observed values at the end of 2008 and remain over the forecast horizon. Accordingly, the adjustments for the no-QE scenario are implemented through a rise in the spreads between the relevant US Treasury yields and the 3-month Treasury bill rate. The no-QE counterfactual simulations for the US Economy are presented in Fig. 5.1.

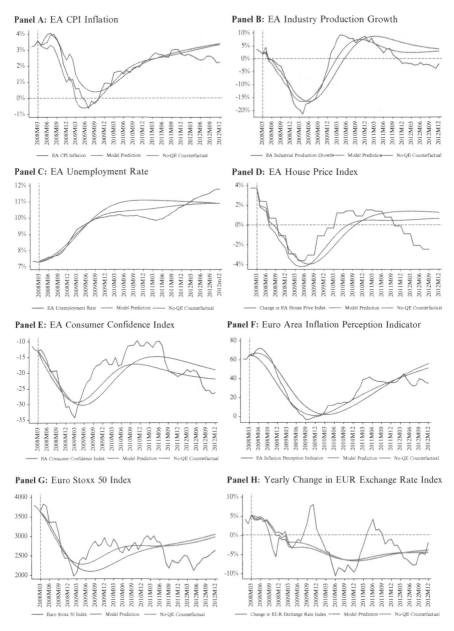

Fig. 5.4 No-QE counterfactual simulations for the Euro Area

Panel A depicts the estimated effect of the Fed's QE on CPI inflation in the USA. It is evident that the model prediction captures the trend in the actual value reasonably well, indicating that the large BVAR model is fairly specified. More importantly, it shows that the no-QE counterfactual lies below the baseline prediction under the QE scenario over the period from the start of QE in the fourth quarter of 2008 to the second quarter of 2010, suggesting that CPI inflation in the USA would have been lower for at least one and a half years if the QE policy had not been implemented. The Fed's QE has a maximum effect of about 1.6 % points on the US CPI inflation, which occurs in the third quarter of 2009, about 9 months after its initial announcement. Therefore, it is found that the Fed's QE does prevent CPI inflation from being more negative, i.e., a deeper deflation of around 4 %, in the USA.

Panel B demonstrates the impact of QE on the US real GDP growth. It shows that the conditional forecasts under QE no-QE scenarios are very close to each other, which indicates that the effect of Fed's QE on the US GDP is negligible. It also shows that the no-QE counterfactual lies above the model prediction in 2010 and 2011, suggesting that output growth in the USA would have been stronger during this period if the unconventional monetary policies had not been undertaken. This result, however, is counterintuitive and is likely due to the cumulative forecast error over a relatively long forecast horizon. Nevertheless, our simulation results suggest that the unconventional monetary policies fail to stimulate economic growth in the USA. An important implication is that monetary policy alone is not enough to reinvigorate economic activities in the wake of the global economic crisis.

Turning to the industrial production growth, Panel C shows that there would have been larger declines in industrial output in the USA during 2009 and 2010 if the QE had not been implemented by the Fed. Specifically, the simulation results suggest that, without QE, the decline in the US industrial production would have been as large as over 15 % in the second quarter of 2009. The maximum effect of the Fed's QE on the US industrial production is estimated to be 2.4 % points in early 2010. Therefore, our counterfactual analysis concludes that, although the Fed's QE fails to boost the US economy as a whole, it to some extent stimulates growth in the industrial sector of the economy.

Apart from achieving price stability and economic growth, another objective of the QE conducted by the Fed is to support progress toward maximum employment. Panel D clearly shows that the unemployment rate in the USA would have been at least half percentage point higher if QE had not been undertaken by the Fed. The impact of QE on the unemployment rate becomes evident by the end of 2009 about 1 year after the launch of the program. Although the gap between the QE baseline prediction and the no-QE counterfactual further widens in 2011 and 2012, it is more likely to reflect the increasing cumulative error as the forecast horizon lengthens, rather than the growing effect of QE.

Panel E illustrates the impact of QE on the expectation about future inflation in the next 12 months. The no-QE counterfactual lies below the model prediction under the QE scenario throughout the forecast horizon, which suggests that the Fed's QE raises expectation toward future inflation over the entire period. The peak effect of 0.55 % point occurs in the third quarter of 2009. The effect of QE on inflation expectation might partially be attributable to the Fed's forward-looking policy guidance. Increases in expected future inflation reduce real yields on Treasury securities, which in turn may help to stimulate current investment and spending.

The impact of QE on the US consumer sentiment is depicted in Panel F. The counterfactual prediction under the no-QE scenario and the model prediction under the QE scenario are closely correlated with each other, trending together with no systematic pattern of one being consistently higher than the other. It is, therefore, suggested that the unconventional monetary policies undertaken by the Fed do not have significant influence on consumer sentiment, and fail to restore confidence in the market.

The counterfactual simulations for the US house price are reported in Panel G. It shows that the actual changes in the US house price observed during this period are rather volatile, and the predicted values from the model do not fit the actual data very well. The no-QE counterfactual for yearly change in the US house price index remains above the model prediction under QE scenario throughout the forecast period, suggesting that the decline in house price would have been smaller in the absence of QE. This is, however, contradictory to the prediction that QE would help boost the house market.

Despite the failure of boosting the house market, Panel H demonstrates that the Fed's QE program manages to support the stock market. The counterfactual analysis suggests that S&P 500 stock price index would have been lower over the period from the end of 2008 onwards if the Fed had not implemented its QE. As the figure shows, the short-term peak effect of QE on stock market occurs in the middle of 2009, with a size of about 70 points or 8 %, while the longer-term effect is even larger. However, given the length of forecast horizon, the longer-term effect of QE on stock market is less informative.

Finally, the counterfactual simulation for the change in the USD exchange rate index is reported in Panel I. It appears that the fitted values, under both the QE and no-QE scenarios, fail to capture the trend in the actual data which is rather volatile over the forecast period. The difference between the no-QE counterfactual and the base prediction is also not obvious, indicating an insignificant effect of QE on the USD exchange rate. It, however, should be noted that the change in the USD exchange rate depend not only on the monetary policy of the Fed at home but also on those of the other major central banks abroad.

Overall, the counterfactual analyses of the Fed's QE using a large BVAR model suggest that, without the set of unconventional monetary policies, there would have been a deeper deflation, larger declines in the US industrial production, a higher unemployment rate, a lower inflation expectation, and a weaker stock market in the USA. However, the estimated effects of the Fed's QE on the US GDP growth, consumer sentiment, house price, and the USD exchange rate are either insignificant or counterintuitive.

5.4.2   Evidence from the UK

For the UK, we assume that, in the absence of the BOE's QE, the 2-, 5-, and 10-year gilt yields would have been 53, 90, and 92 basis points higher than their actual value as observed at the end of the first quarter of 2009. We, therefore, create a no-QE scenario for the UK by implementing these adjustments to the spreads between the relevant UK gilt yields and the 3-month Treasury bill rate over the period from the beginning of the BOE's QE onwards. Figure 5.2 summarizes the no-QE counterfactual simulations for the UK.

Panel A depicts the effect of the BOE's QE on the annual CPI inflation in the UK. Given the changes in the standard rate of UK value added tax (VAT) in recent years which, to some extent, distort the price level,[6] we also plot a constant tax indicator in the figure for comparison purposes. The counterfactual simulation suggests that the BOE's QE is useful in preventing UK CPI inflation from being closer to zero, particularly in the second half of 2009. The peak effect of the BOE's QE on CPI inflation is about 0.7 % point and observed in the first quarter of 2010, about 1 year after the initial launch of QE by the BOE.[7] Panel A also shows that, in the absence of the BOE's QE, the CPI inflation in the UK would have been consistently lower throughout the forecast horizon. The QE policy therefore is effective in helping the UK economy avoid lower inflation or even deflation.

Panel B portrays the counterfactual simulations for the annual real GDP growth rate in the UK. It appears that the compression in gilt yield spreads supports output growth in the UK over the entire forecast period. As the figure shows, the maximum effect of the BOE's QE on the UK real GDP growth reaches about 0.7 % point in the second half of 2010. Therefore, the recovery of the UK economy in the wake of the global economic crisis would have been slower if the central bank had not adopted the unconventional monetary policies.

The impact of the BOE's QE on the economic activities in the UK is further confirmed in Panel C, in which the no-QE counterfactual of the industrial production growth lies consistently below the baseline prediction under the QE scenario. The QE effect on the UK industrial production becomes evident in the early 2010, about 1 year after the QE is undertaken, and remains significant until early 2012. More precisely, the growth in the UK industrial output would have been more than 1 % point lower in the second half of 2010 and the first half of 2011 in the absence of QE. The BOE's QE, therefore, supports the level of UK industrial production and prevents its annual growth rate from being more negative.

Unlike in the USA, maximum employment is not considered as a direct target of the central bank's monetary policy in the UK. The counterfactual simulation for UK unemployment rate is presented in Panel D. It shows that the no-QE counterfactual

---

[6] In response to the recent global economic crisis, the standard rate of VAT in the UK is reduced from 17.5 to 15 % with effect from December 1, 2008 to encourage consumer spending. The cut in VAT is reversed to 17.5 % with effect from January 1, 2010. Following the election in 2010, the new coalition government raises the standard rate of VAT from 17.5 to 20 % with effect from January 4, 2011, in an attempt to tackle the country's record debt.

[7] The maximum effect of the Bank of England's QE on UK CPI inflation would be much greater if it is defined as the difference between the no-QE counterfactual and the actual data, as the model underestimate inflation in the UK over the forecast.

lies below baseline model prediction throughout the entire forecast period, which indicates that, without QE, the unemployment rate in the UK would have been about 0.2 % point lower. This result, however, is counterintuitive since QE are expected to encourage job creation by the private sector.

Panel E depicts the expected future inflation rate as implied by the 5-year index-linked gilt. It shows that the BOE's unconventional monetary policies raise inflation expectation slightly in the UK. The impact of QE on the implied inflation becomes noticeable after more than 1 year of the BOE's initial announcement of its unconventional monetary policy, while the maximum effect of about 0.23 % point occurs in the first quarter of 2011.

As to the UK consumer confidence, the impact of the BOE's QE is rather weak. Panel F shows that the difference between the no-QE counterfactual and the baseline model prediction remains negligible until the end of 2010. The estimated effect of QE on UK consumer confidence remains weak in 2011 and 2012 and becomes less informative as the forecast horizon lengthens. Therefore, the BOE's QE does not raise consumer confidence significantly, and the confidence channel of QE is not effective in the UK.

The counterfactual simulation presented in Panel G suggests that house prices in the UK would have been lower had the BOE not undertaken its unconventional policy measures. The effect of the BOE's QE on the annual change in UK house price index is particularly noticeable in 2010 and 2011, with a maximum effect of 2.1 % points occurs in the third quarter of 2010. Without the BOE's QE, the UK house price recovery in 2010 and early 2011 would have been weaker and shorter.

The impact of the BOE's QE is also reflected in the UK stock market. As shown in Panel H, the no-QE counterfactual lies consistently below the baseline model prediction, which suggests that the unconventional monetary policies, to some extent, support the stock market. However, compared with that in the USA, the effect of QE on stock market in the UK is less significant. The maximum effect of 96 points or 3.8 % occurs in the second quarter of 2010, after more than 1 year of the start of the BOE's QE.

Finally, our counterfactual simulations show that pound sterling would have been slightly weaker if the BOE had not undertaken its QE measures. We do not find empirical evidence that monetary easing leads to depreciation of pound sterling against other major currencies. Again, the changes in GBP exchange rate do not depend solely on the BOE's monetary policies but also on those of the other large central banks in the world.

In summary, the counterfactual simulations for the UK economy suggest that the unconventional monetary policies adopted by the BOE are effective in preventing CPI inflation from being closer to zero or negative, and supporting both the real GDP and industrial production growths in the UK. Meanwhile, our results also indicate that, without QE, there would have been lower levels of inflation expectation and consumer confidence, as well as weaker recoveries in the property and stock markets. The counterfactual simulation results for the UK unemployment rate and GBP exchange rate, however, are counterintuitive.

5.4.3 Evidence from Japan

Our event study results presented in Chap. 4 suggest that the BOJ's unconventional monetary policies reduce JGB yields at 2-, 5-, and 10-year maturities, respectively, by about 14, 26, and 29 basis points. Accordingly, we create the no-QE scenario for Japan's economy by adjusting the relevant JGB yield spreads with respect to the 3-month Treasury bill rate. The decreases in JGB yields, and thus the corresponding JGB yield spreads, are assumed to occur in the initial period of the BOJ's QE and remain throughout the simulation period. The QE counterfactual simulations for Japan's economy are reported in Fig. 5.3.

Panel A depicts the effect of BOJ's unconventional monetary policies on CPI inflation in Japan. Although the BOJ's QE does not compress government bond yields as much as the QE in the USA and the UK does, it prevents CPI inflation in Japan from a deeper deflation. Specifically, our simulations show that the no-QE counterfactual of Japan's CPI inflation lies below the baseline model prediction for the period from the end of 2008 to the second quarter of 2010. It is suggested that, without the BOJ's QE, CPI inflation in Japan would have been about 0.4 % point lower in the second half of 2009. Its maximum effect on CPI inflation occurs about 1 year after the launch of the BOJ's QE.

Panel B illustrates the effect of QE on the real GDP growth in Japan. It seems that the BOJ's QE fails to stimulate the country's economic growth. The difference between the no-QE counterfactual and the baseline model prediction is not noticeable throughout the forecast horizon, which indicates that the real GDP growth in Japan would have been the same even if the central bank had not adopted the series of unconventional monetary measures. The BOJ's QE, therefore, is not effective in terms of stimulating Japan's economy as a whole.

Despite the failure of simulating Japan's GDP growth, Panel C shows that the BOJ's QE plays a role in generating industrial production growth. It appears that the annual growth in industrial output would have been lower for a period of more than 2 years from the beginning of QE to the second quarter of 2011. The effect of BOJ's QE on industrial production growth in Japan is maximized in the second quarter of 2010. The growth rate would have been 2.6 % points lower in that quarter had QE not been undertaken by the central bank.

Panel D demonstrates the impact of the BOJ's QE on Japan's unemployment rate. It shows that, although the impact of the BOJ's unconventional monetary policies is not clear right after their initial introduction, it becomes noticeable after about a year. Specifically, the counterfactual simulations suggest that, in the absence of QE, the unemployment rate in Japan would have been about 0.1 % point higher in 2010 and 2011. Therefore, the BOJ's QE contributes, at least marginally, to the progress toward maximum employment in Japan.

The impact of QE on house prices in Japan is illustrated in Panel E. It clearly shows that the no-QE counterfactual lies well below the baseline model prediction throughout the forecast horizon, which suggests that the fall in house prices in Japan would have been more substantial during this period. The effect of the BOJ's QE on

the annual change in Japan's house price reaches around half percentage point by
the end of 2010 and remains thereafter. Thus, the BOJ's QE, which includes purchases of real estate investment trusts, is effective in supporting house prices in
Japan and preventing them from sharper declines.

Looking at the consumer sentiment in Japan, Panel F indicates that the BOJ's QE
to some extent improves the confidence of participants in the market. Although the
forecasts under both QE and no-QE scenarios do not fit the actual readings of consumer sentiment index very well, the simulation results show that the no-QE counterfactual lies below the baseline model prediction from the end of 2008 to the
beginning of 2012. The potential effect of the BOJ's QE on Japan's consumer sentiment index is as high as two points in 2010.

Since the BOJ's QE also involves the purchases of equities, such as exchange-
traded funds, it is expected to have influence on the Japanese stock market as well.
As shown in Panel G, the no-QE counterfactual of NIKKEI 225 index lies below its
corresponding baseline model prediction throughout the forecast horizon, which
indicates that stock prices would have been lower if the QE had not been undertaken
in Japan. The maximum QE effect of about 500 points or 5.5 % occurs in the second
half of 2009.

The impact of the BOJ's QE on JPY exchange rate, however, is not clear.
As Panel H shows, the no-QE counterfactual of annual change in JPY index lies
below its baseline model prediction before the end of 2010, while lies above it
thereafter. This may indicate that the BOJ's QE supports the value of Japanese yen
in the short run, but encourages JPY depreciation in a longer term. The long-run
effect of QE on JPY exchange rate, however, is less informative given the length of
the forecast horizon.

In a nutshell, Fig. 5.3 shows that, though the BOJ's QE fails to stimulate the
country's real GDP growth, it to certain extent prevents a deeper deflation, encourages industrial production, lowers the unemployment rate, supports house prices,
restores the consumer sentiment, and improves the stock market in Japan.

5.4.4   Evidence from the Euro Area

The empirical results of our event study for the euro area show that the ECB's
unconventional monetary policies reduce EAGB yields at 2- and 5-year maturities
by 14 and 11 basis points, respectively. The EAGB yield at 10-year maturity, however, rises cumulatively by 24 basis points over the set of ECB's QE-related events.
Accordingly, we create a no-QE scenario for the euro area by raising the 2- and
5-year EAGB yield spreads and lowering 10-year EAGB yield spread for the
period from the initial launch of the ECB's unconventional monetary policies in
early 2008 onwards. The no-QE counterfactual simulations for the euro area are
presented in Fig. 5.4.

Panel A depicts the impact of the unconventional monetary policies undertaken
by the ECB on CPI inflation in the euro area. It is evident that the no-QE

counterfactual lies far below the baseline prediction under the QE scenario over the period from March 2008 to the end of 2009, which suggest that the inflation in the euro area would have been much lower or even more negative over this period if the ECB had not implemented its conventional monetary policies. The maximum effect of the ECB's QE on CPI inflation is about 1.6 % points, which occurs in March 2009, around 1 year after its initial announcement. Therefore, the central bank's QE is effective in supporting price stability and preventing a deeper deflation in the euro area.

Panel B illustrates the effect of the ECB's QE on industrial production growth in the euro area. Comparing the no-QE counterfactual and the baseline model prediction shows no systematic pattern of one being consistently higher than the other. Thus, the QE effect on industrial output growth in the euro area is not clear from our simulation results. Given the fact that GDP figures are only available at quarterly frequency, the real GDP variable is not included in the monthly BVAR model for the euro area.

The potential effect of the ECB's QE on the unemployment rate in the euro area is demonstrated in Panel C. Surprisingly, the figure shows that, if the unconventional monetary policies had not been undertaken, the unemployment rate in the euro area would have been lower during the period from late 2009 to the end of 2012, with a maximum effect of 0.6 % point occurs in late 2010. This result is contradictory to the prediction that the unconventional monetary policies would encourage job creation by stimulating private sector investment.

Panel D depicts the QE effect on house prices in the euro area. It shows that the house price index would have been lower in the euro area had QE not been implemented, with the exception for the period from August 2009 to the end of 2010. The effect of the ECB's QE on house prices, therefore, is not clear cut according to our simulation results.

Mixed results are also found for the consumer confidence in the euro area. As shown in Panel E, the no-QE counterfactual lies above the baseline model prediction over the period from March 2009 to September 2010, and lies below the baseline model prediction elsewhere. Therefore, we do not find no solid evidence which shows that the central bank's QE is effective in restoring consumer confidence in the euro area.

Turning to the perceived future inflation, Panel F shows that the ECB's unconventional monetary policies are useful in supporting inflation perception in the euro area, at least in the short run. It is found that the euro area inflation perception indicator would have been much lower in 2008 and 2009 had the unconventional measures not been undertaken. The maximum effect of the ECB's QE on the inflation perception indicator reaches over 15 points at the beginning of 2009, after about 1 year of the start of QE. This effect, however, turns to be less significant over the period from 2010 onwards.

Panel G presents the simulated effect of the ECB's QE on European stock markets. The no-QE counterfactual of Euro Stoxx 50 index lies above its baseline model prediction over the period from the beginning of 2009 to early 2011, indicating that the European stock markets would have been stronger had the unconventional monetary policies not been adopted. This is potentially due to the fact that the unconventional monetary policies taken by the ECB raise interest rates at longer maturities, and thus make bond markets more attractive than stock markets.

Finally, the potential effect of QE on the exchange rate of euro is illustrated in Panel H. It shows that the actual changes in EUR exchange rate index is rather volatile over the forecast horizon, which are not captured by our BVAR model. The difference between the no-QE counterfactual and the baseline model prediction is not apparent, and there is no systematic pattern of one being consistently higher than the other. Thus, the QE effect on the exchange rate of Euro is not significant.

To sum up, the ECB's unconventional monetary policies are effective, at least in the short run, in preventing a longer period of deflation and a lower level of inflation perception. The simulated effect of the ECB's QE on the industrial production, unemployment, house prices, consumer confidence, stock markets, and currency exchange, however, are mixed and inconclusive.

5.5 Conclusion

Overall, our empirical findings presented in this chapter clearly show that unconventional monetary measures taken by the major central banks are effective policy options in supporting price stability in their respective economies. As shown in the simulation results, inflation in these advanced economies would have been lower or more negative if the unconventional monetary policies had not been undertaken. The peak effect of the unconventional monetary policies ranges from 0.4 to 1.6 % points, and typically takes place about 9–12 months after the unconventional monetary policies are taken.

In contrast, our results suggest that the effect of unconventional monetary policies on economic growth is rather limited. No significant effect of QE on GDP growth is found for the major economies, except for the UK where GDP growth would have been as much as 0.7 % point lower if the BOE had not implemented its unconventional monetary policies. Despite the failure of stimulating economic activities as a whole, our simulation results suggest that the unconventional monetary policies to some extent facilitate industrial production growth in the USA, the UK, and Japan.

Besides, it is found that QE also contributes to the reduction in unemployment in the USA and Japan, and the rise in inflation expectation in the USA, the UK, and euro area. Evidence on the QE effect on house prices, stock prices, consumer confidence, and exchange rate, however, are mixed and thus inconclusive. Therefore, monetary policy alone is not enough to solve all the problems. Countries should take extra measures to reinvigorate growth in the wake of the global economic crisis.

Although our counterfactual analyses reveal new insights into the broader economic effect of QE, there are a number of caveats. First, the counterfactual scenarios are constructed by adjusting the spread between relevant government bond yields and the 3-month Treasury bill rate under the assumption that QE affects the macroeconomy solely through their effects on interest rate spreads. Other possible channels through which QE may affect the wide economy are overlooked in these analyses. Second, empirical results presented in this chapter rely heavily on VAR approach, which makes it difficult to interpret in some cases. Since we attempt to comprehensively examine the macroeconomic effect of QE, forecast horizons for the counterfactual simulations are relatively long. As with any VAR model, the forecasts become less informative as the forecast horizon lengthens, and this in turn may reduce the credibility of the simulated QE effect on the economic indicators. In addition, our BVAR results are also subject to the prior information incorporated in the estimations. To overcome this problem, we also estimate our BVARs using non-informative (default) priors, and the results are largely consistent with those reported here. Besides, it is still too soon to judge the effectiveness of the central banks' monetary policies. A longer period of time is needed to better evaluate the full effect of such unconventional measures.

Chapter 6
Conclusion

In this brief, we analyze, theoretically and empirically, the effects of quantitative easing on interest rates and the economy in the USA, Japan, the UK, and Europe. We show the channels through which QE (Quantitative easing) impacts the markets and economy, and develop the central bank loss function and QE game theoretically as a Stackelberg game. Using an event-study methodology, we find that the measures undertaken by the Federal Reserve and Bank of England, which focus primarily on bond purchases, are much more effective in lowering interest rates than those undertaken by the Bank of Japan and the European Central Bank, which have relied more heavily on lending to private financial institutions. Over the QE-related events, government bond yields in the USA and the UK decline cumulatively by over 100 basis points at medium and longer maturities, and more than 50 basis points at shorter maturities. In contrast, an average fall by only about 20 basis points is found for government bond yields in Japan, while mixed results are found for those in the euro area. The different impacts of QE on interest rates across economies, however, should be understood in light of their respective financial system structures.

Although the unconventional monetary policies adopted by the Federal Reserve and Bank of England are similarly designed and both are proven to be effective, our empirical results show that they affect interest rates through distinct transmission mechanisms. Specifically, the decomposition of market responses to the QE-related events suggests that declines in the US Treasury yields largely reflect changes in policy expectations, while declines in UK gilt yields are mainly attributable to the reductions in term premiums. Therefore, the signaling channel is dominant in the QE program conducted by the Federal Reserve, and the portfolio rebalance channel plays a more important role in the conduct of the Bank of England's QE program. The contrasting transmission channels of QE in the USA and the UK are likely to be traced to the differences in their central banks' communication policies. Moreover, this brief reveals new evidence that the signaling channel also plays an important role in the conduct of the Bank of Japan's unconventional monetary policies. This is attributable mainly to the forward guidance policy adopted by the Bank of Japan since it pioneered QE in 2001.

K. Hausken and M. Ncube, *Quantitative Easing and Its Impact in the US,* *Japan, the UK and Europe*, SpringerBriefs in Economics, DOI 10.1007/978-1-4614-9646-5_6, © The Author(s) 2013

Looking at the series of monetary easing during the past few years, our event-study results show that over 80 % of the cumulative changes in government bond yields in the USA and the UK are attributable to the first around of QE undertaken by their central banks. The market responses to the subsequent rounds of QE are much less significant. This brief thus uncovers new insight into the evolution of the unconventional monetary policies' effectiveness. It does seem quantitative easing is losing steam in the USA and the UK. Therefore, extra policy measures are needed to stimulate their economies and keep price stability more effectively.

Using large Bayesian vector autoregression models, we further analyze the impact of QE on the wider economy. Our counterfactual analyses suggest that the unconventional monetary measures taken by the central banks are fairly effective in supporting price stability in their respective economies. The inflation rate in the advanced economies would have been lower or more negative if the unconventional monetary policies had not been undertaken. The peak effect of the unconventional monetary policies on CPI inflation rate ranges from 0.4 to 1.6 % points, and typically takes place about 9–12 months after the unconventional monetary policies are taken.

Our counterfactual analyses also suggest that the effect of unconventional monetary policies on real economic growth is rather limited. No significant effect of QE on GDP growth is found for the major economies, except for the UK where GDP growth would have been as much as 0.7 % point lower if the Bank of England had not implement its unconventional monetary policies. Despite the failure of stimulating economic activities as a whole, our results suggest that the unconventional monetary policies to some extent encourage industrial production in the USA, the UK, and Japan. Besides, our simulations show that the unconventional monetary policies also contribute to the reduction in unemployment in the USA and Japan, and the rise in inflation expectations in the USA, the UK, and euro area. However, evidence on QE's effect on house prices, stock prices, consumer confidence, and exchange rate is mixed and thus inconclusive. It does seem monetary policy alone is not enough to solve all the problems, without some structural reforms and other policy measures.

Although this brief reveals new insights into the unconventional monetary policies undertaken by the major central banks, there are a number of caveats. First, the event studies presented in Chap. 4 focus only on the impact of QE on government bond yields. However, QE may work through various channels and affect different types of assets and their yields in different ways. To better assess the impact of QE, different types of assets, such as corporate bonds and MBSs, should be examined separately. Second, the no-QE scenarios used in our counterfactual analyses are created based on the assumption that QE affects the macroeconomy solely through its effects on interest rate spreads, and thus other possible channels through which QE may affect the wide economy are overlooked. Additional empirical methods therefore should be carried out to confirm our results. Third, it is still too soon to judge the effectiveness of the central banks' monetary policies. A longer period of time is needed to evaluate the full effect of such unconventional measures. This seems to be the case for Japan.

Given the limitations of this brief, further research on the unprecedented quantitative easing is clearly needed. First, it is argued that assets with different characteristics are likely to be affected through different channels, and thus tend to react to QE differently. To better understand the transmission mechanisms of the unconventional monetary policies, we will further investigate the impact of QE on a variety of assets. Second, evaluating the macroeconomic effects of QE is extremely challenging, and the robustness of the results presented in this brief should be further confirmed. We will reexamine the efficacy of the QE programs, preferably, using other empirical methods instead of VARs, in an attempt to illustrate more clearly the relationship between the unconventional monetary policies and their targets. Third, given that the collective magnitude of monetary easing conducted by the major advanced economies may have unintended consequences in other countries, we are also interested in the spillover effects of QE onto emerging economies. Since economies are integrated, the implementation of QE in advanced economies is likely to cause excess flow of liquidity in emerging economies and inadvertently disrupt their currencies, exports, and inflation levels.

Appendix A: Bank of Japan's QE-Related Events Prior to the 2008 Global Economic Crisis

No.	Dates	Event	QE-related announcement
1	March 19, 2001	MPM decisions	BOJ decides to conduct money market operations, aiming at the outstanding balance of the current accounts at around ¥5 trillion
2	August 14, 2001	MPM decisions	BOJ increases the target of the outstanding balance of the current accounts held at the Bank to above ¥6 trillion
3	December 19, 2001	MPM decisions	The Bank decides to increase the outstanding balance of the current accounts to around ¥10 trillion to ¥15 trillion
4	February 28, 2002	MPM decisions	BOJ increases the outright purchase of long-term government bonds from ¥800 billion per month to ¥1 trillion per month
5	September 18, 2002	MPM decisions	The Policy Board introduces the purchase/sale of Japanese government securities with repurchase agreements
6	October 30, 2002	MPM decisions	The Bank decides to conduct money market operations, aiming at the outstanding balance of the current accounts at around ¥15 trillion to ¥20 trillion. The Bank increases its outright purchase of JGBs from ¥1 trillion per month to ¥1.2 trillion per month. The Bank also extends maturities for bills purchased in bill-purchasing operations from 6 months or less to a year or less
7	March 25, 2003	MPM decisions	BOJ decides to conduct money market operations, aiming at the outstanding balance of the current accounts at around ¥17 trillion to ¥22 trillion. BOJ also increases the maximum amount of equity holdings it will purchase from commercial banks
8	April 8, 2003	MPM decisions	The Bank decides to purchase asset-backed securities, including asset-backed commercial papers

(continued)

K. Hausken and M. Ncube, *Quantitative Easing and Its Impact in the US,
Japan, the UK and Europe*, SpringerBriefs in Economics,
DOI 10.1007/978-1-4614-9646-5, © The Author(s) 2013

(continued)

No.	Dates	Event	QE-related announcement
9	May 20, 2003	MPM decisions	BOJ decides to conduct money market operations, aiming at the outstanding balance of the current accounts held at the Bank at around ¥22 trillion to ¥27 trillion
10	October 10, 2003	MPM decisions	BOJ decides to conduct money market operations, aiming at the outstanding balance of the current accounts held at the Bank at around ¥27 trillion to ¥30 trillion
11	February 20, 2004	MPM decisions	BOJ decides to conduct money market operations, aiming at the outstanding balance of current accounts held at the Bank at around ¥30 trillion to ¥35 trillion
12	March 9, 2006	MPM decisions	BOJ decides to change its operating target of money market operations from the outstanding balance of the current accounts at the Bank to the uncollateralized overnight call rate. The first round of BOJ's QE policy is lifted

Source: Authors' summary is based on the information provided by the Bank of Japan (http://www.boj.or.jp/en/announcements/index.htm)

Notes: BOJ and MPM are the Bank of Japan and its Monetary Policy Meeting, respectively

Appendix B: One-Day Changes in US Treasury Yields, OIS Rates, and Yield-OIS Spreads

Event date	Change	1-year	2-year	3-year	5-year	7-year	10-year	20-year	30-year
1. November 25, 2008 (QE1)	Δ(US Treasury yield)	0	−16	−12	−18	−22	−24***	−16	−15
	Δ(OIS rate)	−7	−14	−14	−26	−29	−30	−26	−27
	Δ(Yield-OIS spread)	7	−2	2	8	7	6	10	12
2. December 1, 2008 (QE1)	Δ(US Treasury yield)	−9	−10	−11	−22	−22	−21***	−20	−23
	Δ(OIS rate)	−3	−11	−15	−21	−15	−14	−19	−21
	Δ(Yield-OIS spread)	−6	1	4	−1	−7	−7	−1	−2
3. December 16, 2008 (QE1)	Δ(US Treasury yield)	−5	−10	−14	−16	−15	−16**	−13	−12
	Δ(OIS rate)	−18	−15	−20	−27	−30	−31	−24	−24
	Δ(Yield-OIS spread)	13	5	6	11	15	15	11	12
4. January 28, 2009 (QE1)	Δ(US Treasury yield)	1	2	7	11	11	12**	16	18
	Δ(OIS rate)	5	5	9	11	9	16	18	18
	Δ(Yield-OIS spread)	−4	−3	−2	0	2	−4	−2	0
5. March 18, 2009 (QE1)	Δ(US Treasury yield)	−9	−23	−31	−46	−53	−51***	−34	−26
	Δ(OIS rate)	−4	−11	−20	−27	−36	−39	−32	−29
	Δ(Yield-OIS spread)	−5	−12	−11	−19	−17	−12	−2	3

(continued)

K. Hausken and M. Ncube, *Quantitative Easing and Its Impact in the US, Japan, the UK and Europe*, SpringerBriefs in Economics, DOI 10.1007/978-1-4614-9646-5, © The Author(s) 2013

(continued)

Event date	Change	1-year	2-year	3-year	5-year	7-year	10-year	20-year	30-year
6. August 12, 2009 (QE1)	Δ(US Treasury yield)	−1	−3	−2	1	3	1	9	9
	Δ(OIS rate)	−2	−2	−1	−2	0	1	5	8
	Δ(Yield-OIS spread)	1	−1	−1	3	3	0	4	1
7. September 23, 2009 (QE1)	Δ(US Treasury yield)	−1	−6	−5	−5	−4	−2	0	1
	Δ(OIS rate)	−3	−6	−6	−6	−6	−5	−3	−2
	Δ(Yield-OIS spread)	2	0	1	1	2	3	3	3
8. November 4, 2009 (QE1)	Δ(US Treasury yield)	−2	−1	0	3	4	7	7	7
	Δ(OIS rate)	−2	−4	−2	1	4	4	7	5
	Δ(Yield-OIS spread)	0	3	2	2	0	3	0	2
9. August 10, 2010 (QE1)	Δ(US Treasury yield)	−1	−2	−3	−8	−7	−7	−3	−1
	Δ(OIS rate)	−1	−1	−2	−5	−14	−11	−4	−3
	Δ(Yield-OIS spread)	0	−1	−1	−3	7	4	1	2
10. August 27, 2010 (QE2)	Δ(US Treasury yield)	2	5	6	11	12	16**	16	16
	Δ(OIS rate)	2	5	9	13	18	19	22	22
	Δ(Yield-OIS spread)	0	0	−3	−2	−6	−3	−6	−6
11. September 21, 2010 (QE2)	Δ(US Treasury yield)	0	−4	−5	−9	−11	−11**	−8	−8
	Δ(OIS rate)	−1	−4	−7	−10	−13	−12	−10	−10
	Δ(Yield-OIS spread)	1	0	2	1	2	1	2	2
12. November 3, 2010 (QE2)	Δ(US Treasury yield)	0	0	−2	−4	−2	4	13	16
	Δ(OIS rate)	1	−1	−2	−4	−4	−3	8	9
	Δ(Yield-OIS spread)	−1	1	0	0	2	7	5	7
13. September 21, 2011 (OT)	Δ(US Treasury yield)	2	3	7	3	−3	−7	−13	−17
	Δ(OIS rate)	2	2	1	−2	−5	−8	−14	−17
	Δ(Yield-OIS spread)	0	1	6	5	2	1	1	0

(continued)

(continued)

Event date	Change	1-year	2-year	3-year	5-year	7-year	10-year	20-year	30-year
14. June 20, 2012 (OT)	Δ(US Treasury yield)	2	2	2	3	3	1	1	−1
	Δ(OIS rate)	1	2	1	5	4	4	2	0
	Δ(Yield-OIS spread)	1	0	1	−2	−1	−3	−1	−1
15. August 22, 2012 (QE3)	Δ(US Treasury yield)	−1	−5	−5	−9	−9	−9*	−9	−8
	Δ(OIS rate)	−1	−3	−5	−9	−10	−11	−11	−11
	Δ(Yield-OIS spread)	0	−2	0	0	1	2	2	3
16. September 13, 2012 (QE3)	Δ(US Treasury yield)	−1	−1	−1	−5	−5	−2	1	3
	Δ(OIS rate)	0	−1	−2	−5	−6	−6	−1	1
	Δ(Yield-OIS spread)	−1	0	1	0	1	4	2	2
17. December 12, 2012 (QE3)	Δ(US Treasury yield)	−2	1	0	2	5	6	7	7
	Δ(OIS rate)	0	0	0	3	4	4	5	5
	Δ(Yield-OIS spread)	−2	1	0	−1	1	2	2	2
QE1-related events	Δ(US Treasury yield)	−27	−69	−71	−100	−105	−101	−54	−42
	Δ(OIS rate)	−34	−59	−70	−102	−116	−108	−79	−76
	Δ(Yield-OIS spread)	7	−10	−1	2	11	7	25	34
QE2-related events	Δ(US Treasury yield)	2	1	−1	−2	−1	9	21	24
	Δ(OIS rate)	3	1	1	−1	1	5	20	22
	Δ(Yield-OIS spread)	−1	0	−2	−1	−2	4	1	2
OT-related events	Δ(US Treasury yield)	4	5	9	6	0	−6	−12	−18
	Δ(OIS rate)	3	4	2	3	−1	−4	−12	−16
	Δ(Yield-OIS spread)	1	1	7	3	1	−2	0	−2
QE3-related events	Δ(US Treasury yield)	−4	−5	−6	−12	−9	−5	−1	2
	Δ(OIS rate)	−1	−4	−6	−10	−12	−13	−6	−5
	Δ(Yield-OIS spread)	−3	−1	0	−2	3	8	5	7

(continued)

(continued)

Event date	Change	1-year	2-year	3-year	5-year	7-year	10-year	20-year	30-year
Total net change in US Treasury yield	−25	−68	−69	−108	−115	−103	−46	−34
Total net change in USD OIS rate	−30	−58	−74	−111	−127	−121	−77	−75
Total net change in yield-OIS spread	5	−10	5	3	12	18	31	41

Notes:

All changes are measured in basis points. Cumulative changes may differ from the sum of changes reported for individual events because of rounding

QE1, QE2, and QE3 represent the first, second, and third round of quantitative easing, respectively, and OT represents operation twist

***, **, and * indicate changes in interest rate outside the 0.5th and 99.5th percentile range, the 1st and 99th percentile range, and the 2.5th and 97.5th percentile range of the distribution of interest rate changes in normal time, respectively

Appendix C: One-Day Changes in UK Gilt Yields, OIS Rates, and Yield-OIS Spreads

Event date	Change	1-year	2-year	3-year	5-year	7-year	10-year	15-year	20-year	25-year
1. February 11, 2009 (QE1)	Δ(UK gilt yield)	−23	−30	−29	−26	−23	−21***	−14	−8	−6
	Δ(OIS rate)	−23	−29	−29	−23	−19	−15	−10	−7	−3
	Δ(Yield-OIS spread)	0	−1	0	−3	−4	−6	−4	−1	−3
2. March 5, 2009 (QE1)	Δ(UK gilt yield)	0	−2	−6	−18	−26	−32***	−38	−40	−33
	Δ(OIS rate)	14	8	2	−5	−12	−19	−21	−20	−19
	Δ(Yield-OIS spread)	−14	−10	−8	−13	−14	−13	−17	−20	−14
3. May 7, 2009 (QE1)	Δ(UK gilt yield)	0	2	3	4	5	6	1	−2	0
	Δ(OIS rate)	1	7	10	14	16	16	16	15	13
	Δ(Yield-OIS spread)	−1	−5	−7	−10	−11	−10	−15	−17	−13
4. August 6, 2009 (QE1)	Δ(UK gilt yield)	2	−3	−8	−11	−9	−7*	−10	−14	−16
	Δ(OIS rate)	−8	−9	−6	−1	2	3	2	2	1
	Δ(Yield-OIS spread)	10	6	−2	−10	−11	−10	−12	−16	−17

(continued)

K. Hausken and M. Ncube, *Quantitative Easing and Its Impact in the US, Japan, the UK and Europe*, SpringerBriefs in Economics, DOI 10.1007/978-1-4614-9646-5, © The Author(s) 2013

(continued)

Event date	Change	1-year	2-year	3-year	5-year	7-year	10-year	15-year	20-year	25-year
5. November 5, 2009 (QE1)	Δ(UK gilt yield)	0	1	2	4	6	6	5	4	2
	Δ(OIS rate)	0	−1	0	2	3	5	4	3	2
	Δ(Yield-OIS spread)	0	2	2	2	3	1	1	1	0
6. February 4, 2010 (QE1)	Δ(UK gilt yield)	−1	−2	−3	−2	−2	−1	0	0	0
	Δ(OIS rate)	−3	−10	−7	−5	−7	−4	−3	−2	−2
	Δ(Yield-OIS spread)	2	8	4	3	5	3	3	2	2
7. October 6, 2011 (QE2)	Δ(UK gilt yield)	2	4	4	3	4	4	2	0	−3
	Δ(OIS rate)	3	7	10	7	8	7	5	2	0
	Δ(Yield-OIS spread)	−1	−3	−6	−4	−4	−3	−3	−2	−3
8. February 9, 2012 (QE2)	Δ(UK gilt yield)	1	1	0	−1	0	6	13	16	16
	Δ(OIS rate)	0	−1	−1	1	4	5	8	9	11
	Δ(Yield-OIS spread)	1	2	1	−2	−4	1	5	7	5
9. July 5, 2012 (QE3)	Δ(UK gilt yield)	−2	−7	−9	−9	−7	−6	−3	−2	0
	Δ(OIS rate)	−1	−2	−4	−7	−7	−7	−6	−6	−6
	Δ(Yield-OIS spread)	−1	−5	−5	−2	0	1	3	4	6
QE1-related events	Δ(UK gilt yield)	−22	−34	−41	−49	−49	−49	−56	−60	−53
	Δ(OIS rate)	−19	−34	−29	−19	−17	−15	−11	−10	−8
	Δ(Yield-OIS spread)	−3	0	−12	−30	−32	−34	−45	−50	−45
QE2-related events	Δ(UK gilt yield)	3	5	4	2	4	10	15	16	13
	Δ(OIS rate)	3	6	9	8	11	12	13	11	11
	Δ(Yield-OIS spread)	0	−1	−5	−6	−7	−2	2	5	2

(continued)

(continued)

Event date	Change	1-year	2-year	3-year	5-year	7-year	10-year	15-year	20-year	25-year
QE3-related events	Δ(UK gilt yield)	−2	−7	−9	−9	−7	−6	−3	−2	0
	Δ(OIS rate)	−1	−2	−4	−7	−7	−7	−6	−6	−6
	Δ(Yield-OIS spread)	−1	−5	−5	−2	0	1	3	4	6
Total net change in gilt yield		−21	−36	−46	−56	−52	−45	−44	−46	−40
Total net change in GBP OIS rate		−18	−30	−24	−17	−13	−10	−5	−5	−3
Total net change in yield-OIS spread		−3	−6	−22	−39	−39	−35	−39	−41	−37

Notes:

All changes are measured in basis points. Cumulative changes may differ from the sum of changes reported for individual events because of rounding

QE1, QE2, and QE3 represent the first, second, and third round of quantitative easing, respectively

***, **, and * indicate changes in interest rate outside the 0.5th and 99.5th percentile range, the 1st and 99th percentile range, and the 2.5th and 97.5th percentile range of the distribution of interest rate changes in normal time, respectively

Appendix D: One-Day Changes in Japanese Government Bond Yields, OIS Rates, and Yield-OIS Spreads

Event date	Change	1-year	2-year	3-year	5-year	7-year	10-year	20-year	30-year
1. December 2, 2008 (SFSO)	Δ(JGB yield)	−3	−3	−3	−3	−3	−6*	−4	−6
	Δ(OIS rate)	−1	0	N.A.	N.A.	N.A.	N.A.	N.A.	N.A.
	Δ(Yield-OIS spread)	−2	−3	N.A.	N.A.	N.A.	N.A.	N.A.	N.A.
2. December 19, 2008 (OAP)	Δ(JGB yield)	−5	−4	−3	−3	−2	−3	−3	−5
	Δ(OIS rate)	−2	32	0	N.A.	N.A.	N.A.	N.A.	N.A.
	Δ(Yield-OIS spread)	−3	−36	−3	N.A.	N.A.	N.A.	N.A.	N.A.
3. January 22, 2009 (OAP)	Δ(JGB yield)	0	−1	−2	−2	−1	1	3	2
	Δ(OIS rate)	−2	1	N.A.	N.A.	N.A.	N.A.	N.A.	N.A.
	Δ(Yield-OIS spread)	1	−1	N.A.	N.A.	N.A.	N.A.	N.A.	N.A.
4. February 3, 2009 (OAP)	Δ(JGB yield)	1	1	2	2	2	0	−1	−1
	Δ(OIS rate)	0	0	N.A.	N.A.	N.A.	N.A.	N.A.	N.A.
	Δ(Yield-OIS spread)	1	1	N.A.	N.A.	N.A.	N.A.	N.A.	N.A.

(continued)

K. Hausken and M. Ncube, *Quantitative Easing and Its Impact in the US, Japan, the UK and Europe*, SpringerBriefs in Economics, DOI 10.1007/978-1-4614-9646-5, © The Author(s) 2013

(continued)

Event date	Change	1-year	2-year	3-year	5-year	7-year	10-year	20-year	30-year
5. February 19, 2009 (SFSO/OAP)	Δ(JGB yield)	0	1	−1	−1	0	1	2	1
	Δ(OIS rate)	2	1	N.A.	N.A.	N.A.	N.A.	N.A.	N.A.
	Δ(Yield-OIS spread)	−2	0	N.A.	N.A.	N.A.	N.A.	N.A.	N.A.
6. March 18, 2009 (OAP)	Δ(JGB yield)	0	0	−1	−1	−2	0	1	2
	Δ(OIS rate)	1	0	N.A.	N.A.	N.A.	N.A.	N.A.	N.A.
	Δ(Yield-OIS spread)	−1	0	N.A.	N.A.	N.A.	N.A.	N.A.	N.A.
7. July 15, 2009 (SFSO/OAP)	Δ(JGB yield)	0	1	1	−1	−1	0	0	0
	Δ(OIS rate)	0	0	0	N.A.	N.A.	N.A.	N.A.	N.A.
	Δ(Yield-OIS spread)	0	1	1	N.A.	N.A.	N.A.	N.A.	N.A.
8. October 30, 2009 (SFSO/OAP)	Δ(JGB yield)	1	0	0	0	0	0	0	−1
	Δ(OIS rate)	0	1	0	0	0	1	1	2
	Δ(Yield-OIS spread)	0	−1	0	0	0	−1	−1	−3
9. December 1, 2009 (FRO)	Δ(JGB yield)	−4	−6	−7	−8	−8	−7**	−6	−5
	Δ(OIS rate)	−3	−4	−7	−6	−5	−5	−2	−2
	Δ(Yield-OIS spread)	−2	−2	0	−2	−3	−2	−3	−3
10. December 18, 2009 (PST)	Δ(JGB yield)	−1	−1	−1	−4	−3	−2	−3	−2
	Δ(OIS rate)	0	−1	−1	−1	−2	−2	−3	−4
	Δ(Yield-OIS spread)	−1	1	0	−3	−1	1	0	1
11. March 17, 2010 (FRO)	Δ(JGB yield)	0	0	1	1	2	1	0	1
	Δ(OIS rate)	0	1	1	1	1	2	3	4
	Δ(Yield-OIS spread)	0	−1	1	0	1	−1	−3	−3

(continued)

(continued)

Event date	Change	1-year	2-year	3-year	5-year	7-year	10-year	20-year	30-year
12. April 30, 2010 (GSFF)	Δ(JGB yield)	0	0	1	0	1	0	−1	−2
	Δ(OIS rate)	0	1	0	−1	1	1	1	1
	Δ(Yield-OIS spread)	0	−1	1	1	0	−1	−2	−3
13. May 21, 2010 (GSFF)	Δ(JGB yield)	0	−1	0	−1	−2	−2	−4	−4
	Δ(OIS rate)	0	−1	0	0	−2	−3	−5	−6
	Δ(Yield-OIS spread)	0	0	0	−1	0	1	2	2
14. June 15, 2010 (GSFF)	Δ(JGB yield)	0	0	0	−1	0	0	1	1
	Δ(OIS rate)	0	0	0	−1	0	0	0	0
	Δ(Yield-OIS spread)	0	0	0	0	0	0	0	1
15. August 30, 2010 (FRO)	Δ(JGB yield)	0	0	0	0	1	2	3	3
	Δ(OIS rate)	0	0	−2	0	0	0	4	0
	Δ(Yield-OIS spread)	−1	0	2	1	1	2	−1	4
16. October 5, 2010 (CME)	Δ(JGB yield)	−1	−1	−2	−3	−2	−2	1	1
	Δ(OIS rate)	0	0	−2	−3	−3	−4	−2	−1
	Δ(Yield-OIS spread)	−1	−1	0	0	1	1	3	2
17. October 28, 2010 (CME)	Δ(JGB yield)	0	−1	−1	−2	−3	−4	−1	−2
	Δ(OIS rate)	2	0	1	0	−4	−5	−5	−5
	Δ(Yield-OIS spread)	−2	0	−2	−2	0	1	3	3
18. November 5, 2010 (CME)	Δ(JGB yield)	1	0	1	1	2	1	3	3
	Δ(OIS rate)	0	0	1	1	2	2	2	2
	Δ(Yield-OIS spread)	0	0	0	0	0	−1	1	1

(continued)

(continued)

Event date	Change	1-year	2-year	3-year	5-year	7-year	10-year	20-year	30-year
19. March 14, 2011 (CME)	Δ(JGB yield)	−3	−4	−4	−6	−7	−4	1	2
	Δ(OIS rate)	−2	−5	−4	−5	−5	−4	−2	0
	Δ(Yield-OIS spread)	−1	1	0	−1	−2	0	4	1
20. April 28, 2011 (DA)	Δ(JGB yield)	0	−1	−1	−1	−1	−1	0	0
	Δ(OIS rate)	0	−2	0	−2	−2	−3	−2	−2
	Δ(Yield-OIS spread)	0	2	−1	1	1	2	2	2
21. June 14, 2011 (GSFF)	Δ(JGB yield)	0	0	1	1	2	1	−1	−1
	Δ(OIS rate)	0	0	0	2	1	1	1	1
	Δ(Yield-OIS spread)	0	0	1	−1	1	0	−2	−2
22. August 4, 2011 (CME)	Δ(JGB yield)	0	0	0	1	0	0	0	0
	Δ(OIS rate)	2	0	1	3	0	1	1	2
	Δ(Yield-OIS spread)	−2	0	−1	−2	0	−1	−1	−2
23. October 27, 2011 (CME)	Δ(JGB yield)	0	0	0	1	1	2	2	1
	Δ(OIS rate)	0	0	1	2	2	2	2	2
	Δ(Yield-OIS spread)	0	−1	−1	−1	0	0	0	−2
24. February 14, 2012 (CME)	Δ(JGB yield)	0	−1	−1	−2	−2	−1	0	0
	Δ(OIS rate)	0	−1	3	−1	−2	−3	−2	0
	Δ(Yield-OIS spread)	0	0	−4	0	0	2	1	0
25. March 13, 2012 (GSFF)	Δ(JGB yield)	0	0	0	0	0	0	−1	−1
	Δ(OIS rate)	0	0	0	1	0	0	1	1
	Δ(Yield-OIS spread)	0	0	0	−1	−1	0	−1	−2

(continued)

(continued)

Event date	Change	1-year	2-year	3-year	5-year	7-year	10-year	20-year	30-year
26. April 27, 2012 (CME)	Δ(JGB yield)	0	0	−2	−2	−3	−2	−1	0
	Δ(OIS rate)	0	0	0	−1	−2	−1	−1	−2
	Δ(Yield-OIS spread)	0	0	−1	−1	−1	−1	0	2
27. July 12, 2012 (CME)	Δ(JGB yield)	0	0	0	−1	−2	−1	0	0
	Δ(OIS rate)	0	0	0	−1	−1	−1	−1	−1
	Δ(Yield-OIS spread)	0	0	0	0	0	0	1	1
28. September 19, 2012 (CME)	Δ(JGB yield)	0	0	0	0	1	0	1	1
	Δ(OIS rate)	0	0	0	−1	0	0	1	2
	Δ(Yield-OIS spread)	0	0	0	1	1	1	0	−1
29. October 30, 2012 (CME)	Δ(JGB yield)	0	0	0	0	−2	−1	0	0
	Δ(OIS rate)	0	−1	−1	−1	0	0	0	1
	Δ(Yield-OIS spread)	0	1	1	1	−2	−1	0	−1
30. December 20, 2012 (CME)	Δ(JGB yield)	0	0	0	−1	−1	−1	−1	−2
	Δ(OIS rate)	0	0	0	1	0	−1	−1	−1
	Δ(Yield-OIS spread)	0	0	0	−1	−1	0	−1	−1
31. January 22, 2013 (CME)	Δ(JGB yield)	0	0	0	0	−1	0	0	1
	Δ(OIS rate)	0	2	0	0	2	3	−2	0
	Δ(Yield-OIS spread)	0	−2	0	0	−2	−3	3	0
32. April 4, 2013 (QQME)	Δ(JGB yield)	0	0	0	−1	−5	−11***	−24	−27
	Δ(OIS rate)	0	1	0	−1	−4	−9	−16	−18
	Δ(Yield-OIS spread)	0	0	0	0	−1	−2	−7	−9

(continued)

(continued)

Event date	Change	1-year	2-year	3-year	5-year	7-year	10-year	20-year	30-year
SFSO-related events	Δ(JGB yield)	−2	−2	−3	−4	−4	−5	−3	−5
	Δ(OIS rate)	1	1	N.A.	N.A.	N.A.	N.A.	N.A.	N.A.
	Δ(Yield-OIS spread)	−3	−2	N.A.	N.A.	N.A.	N.A.	N.A.	N.A.
OAP-related events	Δ(JGB yield)	−4	−1	−4	−5	−4	−2	1	−1
	Δ(OIS rate)	−2	33	N.A.	N.A.	N.A.	N.A.	N.A.	N.A.
	Δ(Yield-OIS spread)	−3	−34	N.A.	N.A.	N.A.	N.A.	N.A.	N.A.
FRO-related events	Δ(JGB yield)	−4	−6	−5	−7	−5	−4	−3	−2
	Δ(OIS rate)	−2	−2	−8	−6	−5	−2	5	3
	Δ(Yield-OIS spread)	−2	−4	3	−1	−1	−2	−8	−5
GSFF-related events	Δ(JGB yield)	0	−1	2	0	0	−1	−6	−7
	Δ(OIS rate)	0	0	1	1	0	−1	−3	−3
	Δ(Yield-OIS spread)	0	−1	1	−1	0	0	−3	−5
CME-related events	Δ(JGB yield)	−4	−7	−9	−14	−17	−13	5	5
	Δ(OIS rate)	1	−5	−2	−7	−11	−12	−9	−1
	Δ(Yield-OIS spread)	−4	−2	−8	−7	−7	−2	14	6
Total net change in JGB yield		−16	−20	−22	−35	−38	−40	−34	−41
Total net change in JGB yield (since October 2009)		−9	−15	−14	−27	−31	−32	−31	−34
Total net change in JPY OIS rate (since October 2009)		−1	−10	−10	−16	−24	−30	−29	−24
Total net change in yield-OIS spread (since October 2009)		−8	−5	−4	−10	−8	−3	−2	−10

Notes:

All changes are measured in basis points. Cumulative changes may differ from the sum of changes reported for individual events because of rounding

SFSO represents special fund-supplying operations; OAP represents outright asset purchases; FRO represents fixed-rate operations; PST represents price stability target; GSFF represents growth-supporting funding facility; CME represents comprehensive monetary easing; and SBLF represents simulating bank lending facility

***, **, and * indicate changes in interest rate outside the 0.5th and 99.5th percentile range, the 1st and 99th percentile range, and the 2.5th and 97.5th percentile range of the distribution of interest rate changes in normal time, respectively

Appendix E: One-Day Changes in Euro Area Government Bond Yields, OIS Rates, and Yield-OIS Spreads

Event date	Change	1-year	2-year	3-year	5-year	7-year	10-year	20-year	30-year
1. March 28, 2008 (LTRO)	Δ(EAGB yield)	2	3	4	4	3	2	−1	−2
	Δ(OIS rate)	0	0	1	−2	−2	−2	N.A.	N.A.
	Δ(Yield-OIS spread)	2	3	3	6	5	3	N.A.	N.A.
2. October 15, 2008 (LTRO)	Δ(EAGB yield)	−1	−3	−2	−2	−1	3	17	25
	Δ(OIS rate)	−13	−16	−12	−12	−11	−9	3	6
	Δ(Yield-OIS spread)	12	13	11	10	10	11	14	19
3. May 7, 2009 (CBPP/LTRO)	Δ(EAGB yield)	−3	0	2	5	6	8**	11	12
	Δ(OIS rate)	−3	2	6	11	14	17	16	14
	Δ(Yield-OIS spread)	0	−2	−4	−6	−8	−8	−5	−1
4. June 4, 2009 (CBPP)	Δ(EAGB yield)	8	14	15	14	12	11***	7	5
	Δ(OIS rate)	14	18	19	12	10	8	3	2
	Δ(Yield-OIS spread)	−6	−4	−4	2	3	3	4	3

(continued)

K. Hausken and M. Ncube, *Quantitative Easing and Its Impact in the US, Japan, the UK and Europe*, SpringerBriefs in Economics,
DOI 10.1007/978-1-4614-9646-5, © The Author(s) 2013

(continued)

Event date	Change	1-year	2-year	3-year	5-year	7-year	10-year	20-year	30-year
5. May 10, 2010 (SMP)	Δ(EAGB yield)	−9	−8	−7	−6	−7	−8**	−1	17
	Δ(OIS rate)	0	5	7	8	14	17	26	31
	Δ(Yield-OIS spread)	−10	−13	−13	−14	−21	−25	−27	−14
6. June 30, 2010 (CBPP)	Δ(EAGB yield)	2	2	1	0	−1	−1	0	−6
	Δ(OIS rate)	5	6	4	2	1	0	−1	−2
	Δ(Yield-OIS spread)	−3	−4	−3	−2	−2	−1	1	−5
7. October 6, 2011 (CBPP)	Δ(EAGB yield)	1	−2	−2	−1	−1	−1	−1	−2
	Δ(OIS rate)	11	11	11	9	9	8	8	8
	Δ(Yield-OIS spread)	−10	−13	−14	−11	−9	−9	−10	−9
8. November 3, 2011 (CBPP)	Δ(EAGB yield)	−2	−6	−5	0	5	8**	13	14
	Δ(OIS rate)	−7	−5	−4	−2	2	1	7	−5
	Δ(Yield-OIS spread)	5	−1	−1	2	3	7	6	19
9. December 8, 2011 (LTRO)	Δ(EAGB yield)	2	2	3	2	4	7**	12	13
	Δ(OIS rate)	−1	2	−2	2	−6	−11	−14	−11
	Δ(Yield-OIS spread)	3	0	5	1	10	17	26	25
10. August 2, 2012 (OMT)	Δ(EAGB yield)	0	−1	−4	−8	−6	−1	9	13
	Δ(OIS rate)	2	1	−3	−5	−7	−10	−13	−13
	Δ(Yield-OIS spread)	−2	−2	−1	−3	1	9	23	26
11. September 6, 2012 (OMT)	Δ(EAGB yield)	3	2	−5	−15	−16	−14***	−10	−9
	Δ(OIS rate)	1	3	4	6	8	−2	11	10
	Δ(Yield-OIS spread)	2	−1	−9	−21	−24	−12	−21	−19

(continued)

(continued)

Event date	Change	1-year	2-year	3-year	5-year	7-year	10-year	20-year	30-year
LTRO-related events	Δ(EAGB yield)	−1	3	7	10	12	19	39	49
	Δ(OIS rate)	−17	−12	−8	−2	−5	−4	N.A.	N.A.
	Δ(Yield-OIS spread)	16	14	15	11	18	23	N.A.	N.A.
CBPP-related events	Δ(EAGB yield)	7	8	10	17	22	25	29	24
	Δ(OIS rate)	20	32	36	32	35	34	33	17
	Δ(Yield-OIS spread)	−13	−25	−26	−15	−14	−9	−4	7
OMT-related events	Δ(EAGB yield)	2	1	−9	−22	−22	−15	−1	4
	Δ(OIS rate)	3	4	1	2	1	−13	−3	−4
	Δ(Yield-OIS spread)	0	−3	−10	−24	−23	−2	2	7
Total net change in EAGB yield		2	4	−1	−7	−2	13	54	81
Total net change in EAGB yield (since October 2008)		0	1	−4	−11	−5	11	55	82
Total net change in EUR OIS rate (since October 2008)		9	28	30	31	33	19	45	38
Total net change in yield-OIS spread (since October 2008)		−9	−26	−34	−42	−38	−8	10	44

Notes:

All changes are measured in basis points. Cumulative changes may differ from the sum of changes reported for individual events because of rounding

LTRO represents longer-term refinancing operations; CBPP represents covered bonds purchase programs; SMP represents securities market program; and OMT represents outright monetary transactions

***, **, and * indicate changes in interest rate outside the 0.5th and 99.5th percentile range, the 1st and 99th percentile range, and the 2.5th and 97.5th percentile range of the distribution of interest rate changes in normal time, respectively

Appendix F: Variables for the US BVAR Model

No.	Variable	Transformation	Source
1	US Consumer Price Index (*USCPI*, 2005 = 100)	Log-levels	Federal Reserve Economic Data
2	US Real Gross Domestic Product (*USGDP*)	Log-levels	Federal Reserve Economic Data
3	US Industrial Production Index (*USIPI*, 2007 = 100)	Log-levels	Federal Reserve Economic Data
4	10-Year US Treasury Yield–3-Month Treasury Bill Rate Spread (*TYSPREAD*10)	Levels	Federal Reserve Economic Data
5	5-Year US Treasury Yield–3-Month Treasury Bill Rate Spread (*TYSPREAD*5)	Levels	Federal Reserve Economic Data
6	2-Year US Treasury Yield–3-Month Treasury Bill Rate Spread (*TYSPREAD*2)	Levels	Federal Reserve Economic Data
7	30-Year US Treasury Yield (*TY*30)	Levels	Federal Reserve Economic Data
8	7-Year US Treasury Yield (*TY*7)	Levels	Federal Reserve Economic Data
9	3-Year US Treasury Yield (*TY*3)	Levels	Federal Reserve Economic Data
10	US Federal Funds Rate (*USFFR*)	Levels	Federal Reserve Economic Data
11	6-Month USD Libor (*GBPLIBOR*6)	Levels	Federal Reserve Economic Data
12	3-Month USD Libor–T-Bill Spread (*USDLIBORTB*)	Levels	Federal Reserve Economic Data
13	3-Month USD Libor–US Federal Funds Rate Spread (*USDLIBORFFR*)	Levels	Federal Reserve Economic Data
14	3-Month T-Bill–US Federal Funds Rate Spread (*USTBFFR*)	Levels	Federal Reserve Economic Data
15	US M2 Money Stock (*USM2*)	Log-levels	Federal Reserve Economic Data
16	US M1 Money Stock (*USM1*)	Log-levels	Federal Reserve Economic Data
17	US Unemployment Rate (*USUEMP*, Aged 16+)	Levels	Federal Reserve Economic Data

(continued)

K. Hausken and M. Ncube, *Quantitative Easing and Its Impact in the US, Japan, the UK and Europe*, SpringerBriefs in Economics, DOI 10.1007/978-1-4614-9646-5, © The Author(s) 2013

(continued)

No.	Variable	Transformation	Source
18	US House Price Index (*USHPI*, 1980 = 100)	Log-levels	Federal Reserve Economic Data
19	US Consumer Sentiment Index (*USCSI*, 1966 = 100)	Log-levels	Thomson Reuters/University of Michigan
20	Inflation Expectation (*EXPINF*)	Levels	Thomson Reuters/University of Michigan
21	West Texas Intermediate Oil Price (*WTIOIL*, Dollars per Barrel)	Log-levels	Federal Reserve Economic Data
22	S&P 500 Index (*S&PIND*)	Log-levels	Bloomberg
23	S&P 500 Price-Earnings Ratio (*S&PPE*)	Log-levels	Bloomberg
24	USD Exchange Rate Index (*USDERI*, 1973 = 100)	Log-levels	Federal Reserve Economic Data
25	USD-GBP Exchange Rate (*USDGBP*)	Log-levels	Federal Reserve Economic Data
26	UK Industrial Production Index (*UKIPI*, 2009 = 100)	Log-levels	Office for National Statistics
27	UK Consumer Price Index (*UKCPI*, 2005 = 100)	Log-levels	Office for National Statistics
28	UK Bank Rate (*UKBR*)	Levels	Bank of England

Appendix G: Variables for the UK BVAR Model

No.	Variable	Transformation	Source
1	UK Consumer Price Index (*UKCPI*, 2005 = 100)	Log-levels	Office for National Statistics
2	UK Real Gross Domestic Product (*UKGDP*)	Log-levels	Office for National Statistics
3	UK Industrial Production Index (*UKIPI*, 2009 = 100)	Log-levels	Office for National Statistics
4	10-Year UK Gilt Yield–3-Month Treasury Bill Rate Spread (*GYSPREAD*10)	Levels	Bank of England
5	5-Year UK Gilt Yield–3-Month Treasury Bill Rate Spread (*GYSPREAD*5)	Levels	Bank of England
6	2-Year UK Gilt Yield–3-Month Treasury Bill Rate Spread (*GYSPREAD*2)	Levels	Bank of England
7	20-Year UK Gilts Yield (*GY*20)	Levels	Bank of England
8	15-Year UK Gilts Yield (*GY*15)	Levels	Bank of England
9	7-Year UK Gilts Yield (*GY*7)	Levels	Bank of England
10	3-Year UK Gilts Yield (*GY*3)	Levels	Bank of England
11	UK Bank Rate (*UKBR*)	Levels	Bank of England
12	6-Month GBP Libor (*GBPLIBOR*6)	Levels	Bloomberg
13	3-Month GBP Libor–T-Bill Spread (*GBPLIBORTB*)	Levels	Bloomberg/Bank of England
14	3-Month GBP Libor–UK Bank Rate Spread (*GBPLIBORBR*)	Levels	Bloomberg/Bank of England
15	3-Month T-Bill–UK Bank Rate Spread (*UKTBBR*)	Levels	Bank of England
16	UK M4 Money Stock (*UKM4*)	Log-levels	Bank of England
17	UK M3 Money Stock (*UKM3*)	Log-levels	Bank of England
18	UK Unemployment Rate (*UKUEMP*, Aged 16+)	Levels	Office for National Statistics
19	UK House Price Index (*UKHPI*, 1983 = 100)	Log-levels	Halifax

(continued)

K. Hausken and M. Ncube, *Quantitative Easing and Its Impact in the US, Japan, the UK and Europe*, SpringerBriefs in Economics, DOI 10.1007/978-1-4614-9646-5, © The Author(s) 2013

(continued)

No.	Variable	Transformation	Source
20	UK Consumer Confidence Index (*UKCCI*)	Log-levels	European Commission
21	5-Year Implied Inflation (*IMPINF*)	Levels	Bank of England
22	Brent Oil Price (*BRENTOIL*, Dollars per Barrel)	Log-levels	Bloomberg
23	FTSE All-Share Index (*FTSEIND*)	Log-levels	Bloomberg
24	FTSE All-Share Price-Earnings Ratio (*FTSEPE*)	Log-levels	Bloomberg
25	GBP Exchange Rate Index (*GBPERI*, 2005 = 100)	Log-levels	Bank of England
26	USD-GBP Exchange Rate (*USDGBP*)	Log-levels	Bank of England
27	US Industrial Production Index (*USIPI*, 2007 = 100)	Log-levels	Federal Reserve Economic Data
28	US Consumer Price Index (*USCPI*, 2005 = 100)	Log-levels	Federal Reserve Economic Data
29	US Federal Funds Rate (*USFFR*)	Levels	Federal Reserve Economic Data

Appendix H: Variables for the Japan BVAR Model

No.	Variable	Transformation	Source
1	Japanese Consumer Price Index ($JPCPI$, 2005 = 100)	Log-levels	International Financial Statistics
2	Japanese Real Gross Domestic Product ($JPGDP$)	Log-levels	International Financial Statistics
3	Japanese Industrial Production Index ($JPIPI$, 2005 = 100)	Log-levels	International Financial Statistics
4	10-Year JGB Yield–3-Month Treasury Bill Rate Spread ($GYSPREAD10$)	Levels	Ministry of Finance/Bloomberg
5	5-Year JGB Yield–3-Month Treasury Bill Rate Spread ($GYSPREAD5$)	Levels	Ministry of Finance/Bloomberg
6	2-Year JGB Yield–3-Month Treasury Bill Rate Spread ($GYSPREAD2$)	Levels	Ministry of Finance/Bloomberg
7	20-Year JGB Yield ($GY20$)	Levels	Ministry of Finance
8	15-Year JGB Yield ($GY15$)	Levels	Ministry of Finance
9	7-Year JGB Yield ($GY7$)	Levels	Ministry of Finance
10	3-Year JGB Yield ($GY3$)	Levels	Ministry of Finance
11	Japan Interest Rate ($JPIR$, the Uncollateralized Overnight Call Rate)	Levels	Bank of Japan
12	6-Month JPY Libor ($JPYLIBOR6$)	Levels	Federal Reserve Economic Data
13	3-Month JPY Libor–T-Bill Spread ($YPYLIBORTB$)	Levels	Federal Reserve Economic Data
14	3-Month JPY Libor–Japan Interest Rate Spread ($JPYLIBORIR$)	Levels	Federal Reserve Economic Data/ Bank of Japan
15	3-Month T-Bill–Japan Interest Rate Spread ($JPTBIR$)	Levels	Bloomberg/Bank of Japan
16	Japan M2 Money Stock ($JPM2$)	Log-levels	International Financial Statistics

(continued)

K. Hausken and M. Ncube, *Quantitative Easing and Its Impact in the US, Japan, the UK and Europe*, SpringerBriefs in Economics, DOI 10.1007/978-1-4614-9646-5, © The Author(s) 2013

(continued)

No.	Variable	Transformation	Source
17	Japan M1 Money Stock (*JPM*1)	Log-levels	International Financial Statistics
18	Japan Unemployment Rate (*JPUEMP*, all persons)	Levels	OECD/Statistics Bureau
19	Japan House Price Index (*JPHPI*, 2005 = 100)	Log-levels	OECD
20	Japan Consumer Confidence Index (*JPCCI*)	Log-levels	Cabinet Office
21	Average Oil Price (*AVGOIL*, Dollars per Barrel)	Log-levels	World Development Indicators
22	NIKKEI 225 Index (*NKYIND*)	Log-levels	Bloomberg
23	JPY Real Effective Exchange Rate (*JPYREER*, 2010 = 100)	Log-levels	Bank of Japan
24	USD-JPY Exchange Rate (*USDJPY*)	Log-levels	Bank of Japan
25	US Industrial Production Index (*USIPI*, 2007 = 100)	Log-levels	Federal Reserve Economic Data
26	US Consumer Price Index (*USCPI*, 2005 = 100)	Log-levels	Federal Reserve Economic Data
27	US Federal Funds Rate (*USFFR*)	Levels	Federal Reserve Economic Data

Appendix I: Variables for the Euro Area BVAR Model

No.	Variable	Transformation	Source
1	Euro Area Harmonized Index of Consumer Prices (*EAHICP*, 2005 = 100)	Log-levels	European Central Bank
2	Euro Area Industrial Production Index (*EAIPI*, 2010 = 100)	Log-levels	European Central Bank
3	10-Year EAGB Yield–3-Month Treasury Bill Rate Spread (*EAGBSPREAD10*)	Levels	European Central Bank
4	5-Year EAGB Yield–3-Month Treasury Bill Rate Spread (*EAGBSPREAD5*)	Levels	European Central Bank
5	2-Year EAGB Yield–3-Month Treasury Bill Rate Spread (*EAGBSPREAD2*)	Levels	European Central Bank
6	20-Year EAGB Yield (*EAGBY20*)	Levels	European Central Bank
7	15-Year EAGB Yield (*GY15*)	Levels	European Central Bank
8	7-Year EAGB Yield (*GY7*)	Levels	European Central Bank
9	3-Year EAGB Yield (*GY3*)	Levels	European Central Bank
10	Main Refinancing Operation Rate (*MROR*)	Levels	European Central Bank
11	6-Month EUR Libor (*EURLIBOR6*)	Levels	Federal Reserve Economic Data
12	3-Month EUR Libor–T-Bill Spread (*EURLIBORTB*)	Levels	Federal Reserve Economic Data/European Central Bank
13	3-Month EUR Libor–MRO Rate Spread (*EURLIBORMROR*)	Levels	Federal Reserve Economic Data/European Central Bank
14	3-Month T-Bill–MRO Rate Spread (*EURTBMROR*)	Levels	European Central Bank
15	Euro Area M2 Money Stock (*EAM2*)	Log-levels	European Central Bank
16	Euro Area M1 Money Stock (*EAM1*)	Log-levels	European Central Bank

(continued)

K. Hausken and M. Ncube, *Quantitative Easing and Its Impact in the US, Japan, the UK and Europe*, SpringerBriefs in Economics, DOI 10.1007/978-1-4614-9646-5, © The Author(s) 2013

(continued)

No.	Variable	Transformation	Source
17	Euro Area Unemployment Rate (*EAUEMP*, All Ages)	Levels	European Central Bank
18	Euro Area House Price Index (*UKHPI*, 2010=100)	Log-levels	European Commission
19	Euro Area Consumer Confidence Index (*EACCI*)	Log-levels	European Commission
20	Euro Area Inflation Perception Indicator (*INFPERC*)	Log-levels	European Commission
21	Average Oil Price (*AVGOIL*, Dollars per Barrel)	Log-levels	World Development Indicators
22	Euro Stoxx 50 Index (*STOXXIND*)	Log-levels	Bloomberg
23	Euro Stoxx 50 Price-Earnings Ratio (*STOXXPE*)	Log-levels	Bloomberg
24	EUR Real Effective Exchange Rate (*EURREER*, 1999Q1=100)	Log-levels	European Central Bank
25	USD-EUR Exchange Rate (*USDEUR*)	Log-levels	European Central Bank
26	US Industrial Production Index (*USIPI*, 2007=100)	Log-levels	Federal Reserve Economic Data
27	US Consumer Price Index (*USCPI*, 2005=100)	Log-levels	Federal Reserve Economic Data
28	US Federal Funds Rate (*USFFR*)	Levels	Federal Reserve Economic Data

References

Banbura, M., Giannone, D., & Reichlin, L. (2010). Large Bayesian vector auto regressions. *Journal of Applied Econometrics, 25*(1), 71–92.

Barro, R., & Gordon, D. B. (1983a). A positive theory of monetary policy in a natural rate model. *Journal of Political Economy, 91*(August), 589–610.

Barro, R., & Gordon, D. B. (1983b). Rules, discretion and reputation in a model of monetary policy. *Journal of Monetary Economics, 12*(July), 101–121.

Baumeister, C., & Benati, L. (2010). Unconventional monetary policy and the Great Recession: Estimating the impact of a compression in the yield spread at the zero lower bound (European Central Bank Working Paper Series, No. 1258). Frankfurt am Main, Germany: European Central Bank. Retrieved from http://www.ecb.europa.eu.

Beetsma, R., & Jensen, H. (1999). Optimal inflation targets, "conservative" central banks, and linear inflation contracts: Comment. *American Economic Review, 89*(1), 342–347.

Berkmen, S. P. (2012). *Bank of Japan's quantitative and credit easing: Are they now more effective?* (IMF Working Paper WP/12/2). Washington, DC: International Monetary Fund. Retrieved from http://www.imf.org.

Brandt, P. T., & Freeman, J. R. (2009). Modeling macro-political dynamics. *Political Analysis, 17*(2), 113–142.

Christensen, J. H. E., & Rudebusch, G. D. (2012). The response of interest rates to US and UK quantitative easing. *Economic Journal, 122*(564), F385–F414.

Chung, H., Laforte, J.-P., Reifschneider, D., & Williams, J. C. (2012). Have we underestimated the likelihood and severity of zero lower bound events? *Journal of Money, Credit and Banking, 44*(1), 47–82.

Ciccarelli, M., & Rebucci, A. (2003). *Bayesian VARs: A survey of the recent literature with an application to the European Monetary System* (IMF Working Paper WP/03/102). Washington, DC: International Monetary Fund. Retrieved from http://www.imf.org.

Clarida, R., Gali, J., & Gertler, M. (1999). The science of monetary policy: A new Keynesian perspective. *Journal of Economic Literature, 37*(4), 1661–1707.

Estrella, A. (2005). Why does the yield curve predict output and inflation? *Economic Journal, 115*(505), 722–744.

Fawley, B. W., & Neely, C. J. (2013). Four stories of quantitative easing. *Federal Reserve Bank of St. Louis Review, 95*(1), 51–88.

Gagnon, J., Raskin, M., Remache, J., & Sack, B. (2011). Large-scale asset purchases by the Federal Reserve: Did they work? *International Journal of Central Banking, 7*(1), 3–43.

Hausken, K. (2005). Production and conflict models versus rent seeking models. *Public Choice, 123*(1–2), 59–93.

Hausken, K. (2010). Risk, production, and conflict when utilities are as if certain. *International Journal of Decision Sciences, Risk and Management, 2*(3–4), 228–251.

Hirshleifer, J. (1995). Anarchy and its breakdown. *Journal of Political Economy, 103*(1), 26–52.

Jensen, H. (2002). Targeting nominal income growth or inflation? *American Economic Review, 92*(4), 928–956.

Joyce, M., Lasaosa, A., Stevens, I., & Tong, M. (2011a). The financial market impact of quantitative easing in the United Kingdom. *International Journal of Central Banking, 7*(3), 113–161.

Joyce, M., Tong, M., & Woods, R. (2011b). The United Kingdom's quantitative easing policy: Design, operation and impact. *Bank of England Quarterly Bulletin, 51*(3), 200–212.

Kadiyala, K. R., & Karlsson, S. (1997). Numerical methods for estimation and inference in Bayesian VAR models. *Journal of Applied Econometrics, 12*(2), 99–132.

Kapetanios, G., Mumtaz, H., Stevens, I., & Theodoridis, K. (2012). Assessing the economy-wide effect of quantitative easing. *Economic Journal, 122*(564), F316–F347.

Krishnamurthy, A., & Vissing-Jorgensen, A. (2011). The effects of quantitative easing on interest rates: Channels and implications for policy. *Brookings Papers on Economic Activity, 2011*(Fall), 215–287.

Kurihara, Y. (2006a). Recent Japanese monetary policy: An evaluation of the quantitative easing. *International Journal of Business, 11*(1), 79–86.

Kurihara, Y. (2006b). The relationship between exchange rate and stock prices during the quantitative easing policy in Japan. *International Journal of Business, 11*(4), 375–386.

Kydland, F. E., & Prescott, E. C. (1977). Rules rather than discretion: The inconsistency of optimal plans. *Journal of Political Economy, 85*(June), 473–491.

Lam, W. R. (2011). *Bank of Japan's monetary easing measures: Are they powerful and comprehensive?* (IMF Working Paper WP/11/264). Washington, DC: International Monetary Fund. Retrieved from http://www.imf.org.

Lenza, M., Pill, H., & Reichlin, L. (2010). Monetary policy in exceptional times. *Economic Policy, 25*(62), 295–339.

Litterman, R. B. (1986). Forecasting with Bayesian vector autoregressions: Five years of experience. *Journal of Business and Economic Statistics, 4*(1), 25–38.

Rogoff, K. (1985). The optimal degree of commitment to an intermediate monetary target. *Quarterly Journal of Economics, 100*(4), 1169–1189.

Salop, S. C., & Scheffman, D. T. (1983). Raising rivals' costs. *American Economic Review, 73*(2), 267–271.

Shirai, S. (2013). *Japan's monetary policy in a challenging environment.* Speech at the Bank of Italy and the Eurasia Business and Economics Society Conference, Rome.

Sims, C. (1980). Macroeconomics and reality. *Econometrica, 48*(1), 1–48.

Sims, C. A., & Zha, T. (1998). Bayesian methods for dynamic multivariate models. *International Economic Review, 39*(4), 949–968.

Skaperdas, S. (1991). Conflict and attitudes toward risk. *American Economic Review, 81*(2), 116–120.

Skaperdas, S. (1996). Contest success functions. *Economic Theory, 7*(2), 283–290.

Svensson, L. E. O. (1997). Optimal inflation targets, "conservative" central banks, and linear inflation contracts. *American Economic Review, 87*(1), 98–114.

Svensson, L. E. O., & Woodford, M. (2005). Implementing optimal policy through inflation-forecast targeting. In B. S. Bernanke & M. Woodford (Eds.), *The inflation-targeting debate.* Chicago, IL: University of Chicago Press.

Tullock, G. (1967). The welfare costs of tariffs, monopolies, and theft. *Economic Journal, 5*(3), 224–232.

Tullock, G. (1980). Efficient rent-seeking. In J. M. Buchanan, R. D. Tollison, & G. Tullock (Eds.), *Toward a theory of the rent-seeking society* (pp. 97–112). College Station, TX: Texas A. & M. University Press.

Ueda, K. (2012). The effectiveness of non-traditional monetary policy measures: The case of the Bank of Japan. *Japanese Economic Review, 63*(1), 1–22.

Ugai, H. (2006). *Effects of the quantitative easing policy: A survey of empirical analyses* (Bank of Japan Working Paper Series, No. 06-E-10). Tokyo, Japan: Bank of Japan. Retrieved from http://www.boj.or.jp/en/.

Vestin, D. (2006). Price-level versus inflation targeting. *Journal of Monetary Economics, 53*(7), 1361–1376.

Walsh, C. E. (1995). Optimal contracts for central bankers. *American Economic Review, 85*(March), 150–167.

Walsh, C. E. (2003). Speed limit policies: The output gap and optimal monetary policy. *American Economic Review, 93*(March), 265–278.

Woodford, M. (1999a). Commentary: How should monetary policy be conducted in an era of price stability? In *New challenges for monetary policy*. Kansas City, MO: Federal Reserve Bank of Kansas City.

Woodford, M. (1999b). *Optimal policy inertia* (Working Paper, No. 726 1 August). Cambridge, MA: National Bureau of Economic Research.

Lightning Source UK Ltd.
Milton Keynes UK
UKOW06f0125090715

254811UK00003B/5/P